Shaken by Scandals

Catholics Speak Out About Priests' Sexual Abuse

EDITED BY PAUL THIGPEN

CHARIS

SERVANT PUBLICATIONS
ANN ARBOR, MICHIGAN

Charis Books is an imprint of Servant Publications especially designed to serve Roman Catholics.

Servant Publications Mission Statement
We are dedicated to publishing books that spread the gospel of Jesus Christ, help Christians to live in accordance with that gospel, promote renewal in the church, and bear witness to Christian unity.

Scripture verses are taken from the Revised Standard Version of the Bible, copyrighted 1946, 1952, 1971 by the Division of Christian Education of the National Council of Churches of Christ in the USA. Used by permission.

Excerpts from the English translation of the *Catechism of the Catholic Church* for use in the United States of America copyright 1994, United States Catholic Conference, Inc.—Libreria Editrice Vaticana. Used with Permission.

Servant Publications
P.O. Box 8617
Ann Arbor, MI 48107
www.servantpub.com

Cover design: Alan Furst, Inc. Minneapolis, Minn.

02 03 04 05 10 9 8 7 6 5 4 3 2 1

Printed in the United States of America
ISBN 1-56955-353-X

Library of Congress Cataloging-in-Publication Data

Shaken by scandals : Catholics speak out about priests' sexual abuse / edited by Paul Thigpen.
   p. cm.
 ISBN 1-56955-353-X
 1. Child sexual abuse by clergy. 2. Catholic Church--Clergy--Sexual behavior. I. Thigpen, Thomas Paul, 1954-
 BX1912.9 .S43 2002

2002009023

✦ ✦ ✦

For Eric Patterson—
eternal rest grant unto him, O Lord,
and let perpetual light shine upon him—
and for all the victims and survivors of this horror,
with a prayer for full healing;

also for Msgr. William O. O'Neill,
and all the many holy, faithful priests like him,
with a prayer of gratitude.

Contents

I: Understanding the Crisis

II: Responding to the Crisis

III: Scripture Readings, Reflections, and Prayers

IV: Responses from Church Officials

"So Much Pain, So Much Sorrow"

An Introduction

The images are haunting—portraits of innocence defiled, childhood stolen, faith shattered.

A small boy, left alone all day in a ramshackle house in the middle of nowhere, without food or heat on a bitterly cold winter's day—a boy trembling, not just from the cold but in terror of the priest who had left him there in a rage for daring to resist his sexual advances.

A woman in her middle years, assaulted by a priest repeatedly when she was a preschooler, who still shudders at the sight of a priest or nun and remembers vividly the cross that dangled over her face, hanging from her abuser's neck, as he raped her.

A young man, emaciated, anguished, pounding his head against the tile floor in a hospital psychiatric unit, wrestling with demons that had tormented him since he was twelve, when a priest sexually abused him—a young man who finally took his own life.

Some kept their suffering a secret for decades, too ashamed to tell. Others tried to tell but were dismissed or intimidated by Church officials into silence. Now at last—thanks largely to the secular press, the courts, and the courage of abuse survivors—the dike of secrecy has broken, and the horror stories are flooding out.

We know now about countless children and youth molested in Catholic schools, rectories, monasteries, convents, seminaries, summer camps, confessionals—even, God help us, beside altars where the Most Holy Sacrifice is offered.

We know as well about bishops taking part in the abuse, some directly, others indirectly by covering it up to protect the predators and their own reputations, bullying and silencing the victims, and shuffling the criminals to new positions where they repeated their unspeakable abominations.

No doubt there are more revelations, perhaps many more, to come.

Fundamental Questions

As the sins of the clergy are publicly exposed, the Catholic Church in America finds itself in crisis. Catholics across the country, shaken and outraged, seem to be asking two fundamental questions: How could this happen? What can we do about it?

This collection is an attempt by a handful of loyal Catholic observers to address these questions with clarity, charity, and forthrightness—to "speak the truth in love" as they see it (see Eph 4:15). Pope John Paul II has rightly called the current crisis a "complex and difficult situation." It merits, then, a complex and thoughtful response. By bringing together the insights and experiences of Catholics from a wide array of backgrounds, we hope to provide such a response—rich in its variety of perspectives and complex in its simultaneous focus on various aspects of the situation that deserve our attention.

The contributors include journalists, priests, leaders of lay apostolates, a parent, a psychotherapist, a moral theologian, a social/political analyst, and a Church historian. Not surprisingly, their approaches to the subject are as diverse as their backgrounds and concerns, encompassing the personal and the analytical, the devotional and the clinical, the pastoral and the theological, the journalistic and the historical.

The authors in these pages would not all agree in every respect on the sources of the crisis nor on what should be done to resolve it. They would debate such issues as these: Have factors inside the Church or outside it had the more corrosive effect on sexual morality among the clergy? Is homosexual orientation sufficient reason to reject a candidate for priestly ministry? Does the Church need a zero tolerance policy for clerical sexual offenders—and if so, what exactly do we mean by "zero tolerance"? Should the bishops and other Church officials who have mishandled the situation resign?

Nevertheless, these writers do agree on a number of fundamental issues, and in their agreement they distinguish themselves from the many commentators who seem eager to "solve" the difficulty by dissolving the Tradition of the Church. What emerges clearly from this volume as a whole, then, is the firm conviction that to purify and reform itself, the Church must become *more* Catholic, not *less*. To paraphrase Chesterton, the problem is not that the Tradition has been tried and found wanting; rather, it has been found too demanding, and not tried.

Specific Issues Addressed

The first section of the book, "Understanding the Crisis," begins with an overview by a journalist who is well situated to provide that perspective: Philip Lawler, editor of *The Catholic World Report*. Inevitably, related events have continued to unfold even in the few days since his account was written, but it is nevertheless a useful summary that provides context for commentary and analysis in the essays that follow.

Next comes a letter from Fr. Joseph F. Wilson, a priest of the diocese of Brooklyn, whose passionate account of his disturbing experience in the seminary and beyond compels us to think carefully about the sources of the crisis. Though we were unable to include in this collection, as we had hoped to do, a profile of Eric Patterson—one of the victims—Fr. Wilson's essay also introduces us to some specifics in the tragic story of this young man and his family, putting a human face on the numbing statistics of abuse.

The roots of the crisis are further explored in the next four essays. Mark Lowery, associate professor of moral theology at the University of Dallas, analyzes problems in the formation of seminarians in light of Pope John Paul II's encyclical letter *Veritatis Splendor*. Michael Novak, director of social and political studies at the American Enterprise Institute, examines what role so-called "progressive" teachers within the Church have played in creating the moral chaos now evident to all. Raymond Arroyo, news director for Eternal Word Television Network (EWTN), responds to the common perception that clerical celibacy is somehow responsible for the problem. And *National Review* columnist Rod Dreher, with characteristic courage, tackles a subject at the heart of the scandal that many in the secular media have tried so hard to ignore: the connections between clerical sexual abuse and the gay subculture.

Section II, "Responding to the Crisis," starts with the concern that should be foremost in the minds of all involved: How do we help the victims? Psychotherapist Gregory Popcak, director of the Pastoral Solutions Institute, provides clinical and pastoral insights here.

Clearly, the American episcopacy must bear a large share of the burden of reform. In an open letter to the bishops, the editors of *The Catholic World Report* lay out their vision of what needs to be done. Journalist Mark Shea follows with the kind of straightforward, feisty analysis for which he is well known, along with remarks about some helpful and not-so-helpful ways for Catholics to respond to the scandals.

After the victims and their loved ones, perhaps the people most unjustly damaged by these scandalous crimes are the countless faithful priests who now appear in public under a cloud of suspicion and shame because of the sins of their brothers. Fr. Mitch Pacwa, known by many Catholics for his thoughtful commentary on EWTN broadcasts, speaks from firsthand experience about the challenges faced by innocent clergy, who must take up the cross of undeserved humiliation, maintain personal sexual integrity, and continue to serve the Church and the world with joy.

A spiritually lethal fallout of cynicism has spread out from the scandals to touch many, including some Catholic children old enough to understand something of what has happened. Kristine Franklin, a parent of two, whose popular books for young people have inspired countless readers, urges families to counteract the fallout by seizing the moment to teach children about sin, grace, redemption, and hope.

Non-Catholics, too, have felt from a distance the unpleasant effects of the scandals, prompting questions and critiques. Al Kresta, the CEO of Ave Maria Communications, is known for his thoughtful Catholic apologetics and lively syndicated radio talk show; he offers useful advice on how to discuss the matter with those outside the Church.

Even among Catholics, the remarkable breadth and depth of the problem faced by the Church can lead to anger, discouragement, and a sense of powerlessness. Leon Suprenant, president of the lay apostolate Catholics United for the Faith, offers the encouragement that God can bring good out of even the greatest evils. He suggests eight practical steps for Catholic laymen and women to become part of the solution by cooperating with divine grace.

Finally, no collection such as this one would be complete without at least a few insights from history on the subject at hand. Americans tend toward historical myopia, often getting caught up in the sensations of daily headlines without much awareness of how current events fit into a bigger, longer picture. Such nearsightedness is especially lamentable among American Catholics, who can draw on the wisdom of a two-thousand-year-old institution. The second section of essays concludes, then, with a few lessons from Church history offered by the editor.

A Situation in Flux

Of course, to speak of the collection as being in any sense "complete" is misleading. God alone knows what surprising revelations might develop in the coming months, what bishops might resign, what invisible forces at work might soon emerge into the light of day, for better or for worse. Lawsuits and claims of abuse continue to multiply, rumors abound, and the evil compounds itself in suicides and other fresh outbreaks of violence.

Yet there are hopeful developments as well. The truth is coming to light. Justice is waking from her long, fitful sleep as some of the perpetrators face up at last to their crimes. Abuse survivors speak of finding new hope for healing. Lay groups such as Catholics for Authentic Reform are emerging to offer insights from the pew.

Of critical significance are the bishops' plans for reform. These are necessarily a work in progress and subject to continuing debate, but they have made a start. In a special section at the end of the book, we have included several texts that document some Church officials' responses to the crisis, along with remarks from the Holy Father. Though we were unable to include here the documents produced by the American bishops at their annual meeting in Dallas, those texts are available online at the USCCB website, www.nccbuscc.org.

If the situation remains in such flux, some might ask, why not wait a little longer—until things "settle down"—to publish a book on the topic? The point is well taken. And yet the truth is that the situation may well continue unsettled for a long time, with stories developing for years. Even books that come out much later will have to close with the caveat, "This is the situation thus far."

Meanwhile, public interest in the scandals is strong; American Catholics, though disgusted, have not yet wearied of the subject, and many opinions and policies have yet to be formed. What better time than now to contribute to the national conversation?

No Solutions Without Prayer

In one final respect, this collection differs from most other books on this crisis that are now appearing: It includes a section of scriptural texts, reflections, and prayers. No genuine solution to the problems facing the Church will be found without a profound turning to God by his people in sincere, soul-searching, persistent prayer. All the better if that prayer is shaped by the wisdom of the Scripture and tradition. As Pope St. Gregory the Great once said to his fellow bishops assembled in council: "The matters we have called to your attention will be fulfilled better through prayer than through discussion. Let us pray."

Any urge to supply commentary in this section has been resisted. The biblical texts are the Word of God, and the reflections are the words of those who know God. They speak for themselves. As for the prayers, they have been gathered from a number of sources, with a few more written especially for the needs of the moment. If they supply even just a starting point for the intercession the Church desperately needs, then their purpose will be fulfilled.

As we pray, we do well to keep in mind what the Holy Father told the American cardinals when they met in Rome to address the crisis: "We must be confident that this time of trial will bring a purification of the entire Catholic community.... So much pain, so much sorrow must lead to a holier priesthood, a holier episcopate, and a holier Church."

To these words of hope—a hope utterly necessary if we are to persevere in transforming prayer and effective action—all the contributors to this little volume would add their fervent *Amen.*

Paul Thigpen
Feast of the Most Sacred Heart of Jesus

I: Understanding the Crisis

ONE

Priestly Misconduct, Episcopal Neglect
An Overview of the Scandals

Philip F. Lawler

If the scandal caused by clerical sex abuse eventually leads to reform and renewal in the Catholic Church in America, as I hope and pray it will, then history will record that the Catholic restoration was sparked, ironically enough, by the *Boston Globe*—a newspaper with a long history of hostility toward the Church.

The scandal had been spreading for nearly twenty years, like some flammable liquid leaking from a massive container, before the *Globe* supplied the spark that caused the explosion. In 1984, American Catholics were horrified to learn that a Catholic priest in Louisiana, Gilbert Gauthe, had been indicted for sexual assault on dozens of adolescent boys. Their horror grew as other, similar cases emerged. Rudy Kos in Texas and James Porter in Massachusetts had—like Gauthe—molested scores of boys over a period of years. Still worse, there was ample evidence that these predator-priests had been allowed to continue in parish work long after their ecclesiastical superiors learned of their misconduct.

Gauthe, Kos, and Porter were eventually jailed for their sexual misconduct. But their victims claimed that the guilty priests' diocesan superiors, too, bore some responsibility for the crimes. Some brought suit against the dioceses in which these priests had served, charging that the bishops' neglect had contributed to the problem. In the most dramatic lawsuit, a Texas court ordered the Dallas diocese to pay $120 million in damages to the victims of Rudy Kos. (Since the judgment far exceeded the resources of the diocese, the victims later agreed to accept roughly one-fourth of that sum.)

While these few spectacular cases commanded the headlines, there were many others. In his 1993 book *Lead Us Not Into Temptation,* Jason Berry reported: "Between 1983 and 1987, more than two hundred priests and religious brothers were reported to the Vatican embassy for sexually abusing youngsters, in most cases teenage boys—an average of nearly one accusation a week in those four years alone."

Many of these assaults, too, resulted in lawsuits; in most cases they were settled quietly, with dioceses approving financial compensation for the victims. Yet the consistent pattern of the cases—a pattern of priestly misconduct and episcopal neglect—was a frightening one. Berry quoted Fr. Thomas Doyle, O.P., a canon lawyer who had worked for the papal nuncio, as saying that the sex-abuse scandal was "the most serious problem that we in the Church have faced in centuries."

2002: The Explosion

Still, Fr. Doyle's judgment was a distinctly minority opinion until January 2002. Then the *Boston Globe*—having obtained a court order to release the relevant documents—published a detailed description of the case of another serial molester, John Geoghan. The *Globe's* investigative report, buttressed by dozens of letters and memos from the files of the Boston archdiocese, showed that Cardinal Bernard Law and his predecessor Cardinal Humberto Medeiros had responded to Geoghan's repeated offenses by shuffling him off to new parish assignments. Occasionally the troubled priest had been sent off to a treatment facility, but never had parishioners been warned that he might constitute a danger to their children.

Perhaps most galling of all, when Geoghan had finally been forced into retirement, Cardinal Law had written him a warm letter, thanking him for his years of service. No such personal solicitude had been shown to the simple Catholic parishioners who had warned the cardinal about Geoghan's activities. The *Globe* report exposed an attitude of rampant clericalism in the Boston archdiocese; the predator priest had been accorded more sympathy and protection than the innocent children.

The exposure of the Geoghan case confirmed the worst fears of those who had been watching the sex abuse story unfold for a decade or more. Loyal Catholics had been reluctant to believe what some cynical reporters hinted: that their bishops might prefer to leave children exposed to physical and spiritual danger, rather than expose the misdeeds of a corrupt cleric. Here they were confronted with documentary evidence that the cynics had been right.

Now the sex-abuse story took on new momentum. Following the *Globe*'s example, media outlets in other cities began to press for details about the known cases of priestly misconduct. Law enforcement officials launched their own investigations, demanding cooperation from chancery officials and asking for the release of diocesan personnel records. An avalanche of new allegations began, with literally thousands of people coming forward to charge that they had been molested by priests.

In response to mounting public pressure, American dioceses began to remove pastors who had been accused of sexual misconduct; these cases added to the clutter of headlines. Catholic parishioners all across the country learned, to their dismay, that their dioceses had already reached out-of-court settlements with men who had reported being molested by priests. In the Boston archdiocese alone, nearly a hundred priests were identified as accused sex offenders; the quiet settlement of lawsuits had already drained millions of dollars from the archdiocesan coffers. New accusations were leveled, new lawsuits were filed. By late March, the sex abuse scandal had become the fodder for daily headlines in newspapers all across the United States.

Although the news was uniformly grim, and the American bishops were unmistakably on the defensive, their supporters could still muster some plausible arguments on their behalf. Although it was now clear that bishops had not acted decisively to remove priests who threatened children, their supporters argued that Church leaders were guilty of nothing worse than a tragic mistake. The bishops had not realized that pedophilia is usually incurable, they argued. Their decision to leave priests in parish assignments, even after reports of sexual misconduct, had been motivated by a deadly combination of compassion and inaccurate information.

Then American Catholics were shaken by a new explosion.

Boston: Ground Zero

Once again "ground zero" was in Boston. At a press conference there on April 8, an attorney representing sex abuse victims made public a new set of documents showing that officials of the Boston archdiocese had advanced the career of Fr. Paul Shanley despite that priest's record of pedophilia. Shanley had not only admitted to sexual activities with young men; he also had written columns for gay newspapers *advocating* sex with adolescents, spoken to a meeting of the North American Man-Boy Love Association, and operated a bed-and-breakfast catering to gay couples.

Finally, after a series of incidents stretching over twenty years, the Boston archdiocese had removed Shanley from his "street ministry." Yet even then, the archdiocese had assured Church officials in California that they had no reason to worry about the priest's background when Shanley moved to the West Coast. One archdiocesan official had volunteered advice on how Shanley might evade the pursuit of a man who had lodged sex abuse complaints against him. Cardinal Law himself actually wrote a recommendation for Shanley—again making no mention of his history of pedophilia—for a position as director of a hostel serving young people in New York.

Already under fire because of the Geoghan case, Cardinal Law came under savage criticism now in the wake of the Shanley revelations. Several prominent columnists had already called for his resignation. On April 11 a rumor ripped through Boston media circles that the cardinal had sent a fax message to the papal nuncio in Washington, indicating that he was prepared to step down. Reporters clustered around the cardinal's residence in a grim vigil, waiting for an announcement.

Unknown to the press, while the reporters were gathering outside his door, Cardinal Law had slipped out of town and was on his way to Rome. He returned to Boston—surprising the reporters who thought he had been sequestered in his residence—and announced that he had met with Pope John Paul II, who had encouraged him to continue his work in Boston.

Rome: Emergency Meetings

During that same weekend, coincidentally, the leaders of the U.S. Conference of Catholic Bishops (USCCB) had also been in Rome for meetings with Vatican officials. (They, too, had been unaware of Cardinal Law's secret trip to Rome.) The visit by USCCB officials had been a routine event, planned well in advance. But under the circumstances, their meetings with Vatican officials took on special importance—a fact that was underlined when Pope John Paul invited the American bishops to meet with him over lunch.

Before flying back to the United States, the USCCB president, Bishop Wilton Gregory, held a special briefing for the media in Rome. Bishop Gregory assured the assembled reporters that the Holy Father was counting on the U.S. bishops to handle the sex abuse scandal by themselves.

Within forty-eight hours after Bishop Gregory's confident statement, reporters learned that the Vatican was not prepared to let the scandal run its course in America. The Vatican had summoned all the American members of the College of Cardinals—and, apparently as an afterthought, the leaders of the USCCB—for an emergency meeting at the Vatican.

In the days leading up to that special meeting, several American prelates indicated that they would urge the Vatican to consider fundamental reforms, such as an end to the discipline of priestly celibacy and possibly even the ordination of women. One cardinal, speaking anonymously to the *Los Angeles Times*, said that the American delegation would lobby heavily for the resignation of Cardinal Law.

When they arrived in Rome, however, the U.S. bishops found that Vatican officials had different issues on their minds. The Vatican had not summoned the American prelates to hear their suggestions; Rome did not need advice from the bishops who had presided over the American debacle. This meeting would focus on what the U.S. bishops should do—belatedly—to restore discipline in the American Church.

Addressing the American prelates on the first day of their meeting, Pope John Paul told them:

> It must be absolutely clear to the Catholic faithful, and to the wider community, that bishops and superiors are concerned, above all else, with the spiritual good of souls. People need to know that there is no place in the priesthood and religious life for those who would harm the young. *They must know that bishops and priests are totally committed to the fullness of Catholic truth on matters of sexual morality,* a truth as essential to the renewal of the priesthood and the episcopate as it is to the renewal of marriage and family life (*emphasis added*).[1]

Quickly picking up the cues, the American bishops stopped talking to reporters about celibacy and women's ordination. Cardinal Roger Mahony of Los Angeles (widely believed to be the unnamed prelate who had told the *Los Angeles Times* about the movement for Cardinal Law's resignation) told the press that there had been no discussion at all about the Boston prelate's situation.

When the two-day meeting ended, the Vatican officials and U.S. bishops approved a joint statement that provided a clear mandate for action by the American hierarchy. The statement read, in part:

Given the doctrinal issues underlying the deplorable behavior in question, certain lines of response have been proposed:

a) the pastors of the Church need clearly to promote the correct moral teaching of the Church and publicly to reprimand individuals who spread dissent and groups which advance ambiguous approaches to pastoral care....

b) a new and serious apostolic visitation of seminaries and other institutes of formation must be made without delay, with particular emphasis on the need for fidelity to the Church's teaching, especially in the area of morality, and the need for a deeper study of the criteria of suitability of candidates to the priesthood.[2]

What the American Bishops Face

A forthright response to that mandate from Rome would force the U.S. bishops to confront some powerful forces within American society, and even within their own hierarchy. Are the bishops ready to wrestle with an increasingly powerful gay rights movement, a struggle that would be provoked by acknowledging that the sex abuse scandal revolves primarily around homosexual activity? Are they willing to investigate reports of an influential homosexual network within the Church?

Will bishops allow full disclosure of the facts in sex abuse cases, rather than continuing to push for the quiet settlement of claims? Will they recognize that sexual misconduct is the next logical step after the tacit acceptance of widespread dissent from Church teachings on sexual morality? Will the proposed apostolic visitation be a rigorous, independent look at seminary life?

As this essay is written, two weeks prior to the bishops' meeting, the answers to those questions are still not clear. What is abundantly clear, however, is the need for decisive action to address this scandal. It is nearly impossible, at this moment, to provide any accurate statistics regarding the scope of the sex abuse problem, with new cases emerging by the dozens every day. But even a rough accounting shows that Fr. Doyle was not exaggerating when he said that this is "the most serious problem that we in the Church have faced in centuries."

In the United States alone, several thousand priests have been accused of sexual misconduct, by tens of thousands of alleged victims. The lawsuits filed by those victims have already forced American dioceses to pay out hundred of millions of dollars in damages; lawyers estimate that the payments will eventually run into the billions and drive some dioceses into bankruptcy.

At least six U.S. bishops have been forced to resign in the past five years after allegations of sexual misconduct. (In the most egregious case, in Palm Beach, Florida, Bishop J. Keith Symons stepped down in 1998 amid allegations of affairs with young men; his successor, Bishop Anthony O'Connell, resigned in 2002 for the same reason.) Two bishops have reportedly made six-figure payments, drawn on diocesan funds, to stave off lawsuits threatened by men who claimed that the bishops had sexually assaulted them. One of those bishops, Rembert Weakland of Milwaukee, has resigned.

American Catholics have no monopoly on the sex abuse scandals. The same charges that now dog the U.S. bishops have also prompted the resignation of a bishop in Ireland, an archbishop in Poland, a cardinal in Austria. But nowhere else has the problem been shown to be so widespread as it is in the United States; nowhere else has the press scrutiny been so relentless.

In the light of that scrutiny, the disturbing revelations will no doubt continue to multiply in the days to come. How will American Catholics, both clergy and laity, respond? God grant that they consider the matter carefully, for their response may shape the course of the Church in America for a long time to come.

✦

Philip F. Lawler is editor of the monthly magazine Catholic World Report *and the online daily service* Catholic World News *(cwnews.com). His work as a journalist and columnist has appeared in over two hundred newspapers in the U.S. and abroad.*

---

1. See "Address of Pope John Paul II to the Cardinals of the United States and Conference Officers," April 23, 2002, pp. 209-11 of this volume.

2. See "Final Communiqué of the American Cardinals at Rome," pp. 213-17 of this volume.

TWO

The Enemy Within
MTV Is Not the Problem

Fr. Joseph F. Wilson

In the current crisis caused by revelations of clerical sexual abuse, we have to be careful not to misidentify the source of the problem. Some observers insist on blaming the corrosive effects of immorality in the secular culture. No doubt the sickness that currently afflicts our sex-saturated society is obvious to anyone who has eyes to see and ears to hear. Sexually explicit imagery does indeed surround us through every possible medium and is used to sell everything from cars to toothpaste. It is indeed true that neither the Church nor the priesthood exists in a vacuum, and it is foolish and unrealistic to expect that either will be unaffected.

But before we point the accusing finger at the pernicious influence of MTV, it would be helpful if we were honest and humble about our own failings as a Church. Just take a look at the new book by Michael Rose, *Goodbye, Good Men.* It is a careful but searing description of the lamentable, sordid state of most of our seminaries—page after page of stories and situations that most lay people would find literally unbelievable, but which I and anyone who has been through the seminary in the last quarter century know to be all too true. If anything, Mr. Rose was restrained.

Thousands of idealistic young men have presented themselves to the Church for formation in the past thirty years. Most of them found themselves consigned by their bishops to a situation in which the theology they received was at best questionable and often dissenting; in which the moral teachings of the Church were undermined, often not subtly at all; in which discipline was lax to virtually nonexistent, spiritual formation wholly inadequate, and immoral and scandalous situations frequently encountered.

Seminary Experience in Dallas

I was in the seminary from 1977 to 1986. The theologate from which I graduated was the Dallas seminary. Under the influence of the vice rector in charge of the collegians there, the college wing of the seminary deteriorated dramatically, discipline eroded, sexually scandalous situations proliferated, and good men abandoned their vocations in disgust. That vice rector left the priesthood a year after I graduated—to "marry" the president of the Dallas Gay Alliance. He thoughtfully invited the seminarians to the festivities.

He had been our moral theology professor (he had studied for his doctorate in moral theology at the local Methodist university). In his class we used Fr. Andre Guindon's text, *The Sexual Language*. This was a fascinating work, in the pages of which I learned, for example, that gay sex is in some ways preferable to straight sex because it is more innovative, expressive, playful. It is interesting to look back and see how many of the men in that seminary left, either before or after ordination, to embrace an active homosexual lifestyle, often with each other.

I actually had the experience of sitting through a lecture by Fr. Paul

Shanley, the Boston priest who was recently arrested in California. As the public now knows, the Boston chancery office had a file of sixteen hundred pages on Fr. Shanley, including the diaries in which he described teaching kids how to shoot up drugs and letters from all over the country protesting the lectures he gave in which he actively promoted pedophilia as helpful and healthy. The lecture I heard was for the priests of the Dallas diocese and for the third- and fourth-year seminarians. I was sitting directly behind the then bishop of Dallas, Thomas Tschoepe, who laughed and joked his way through a truly vile presentation.

This was part of my formation for the sacred priesthood. I faced other problems in that process as well: In my first year of theology, for example, almost all our textbooks were paperbacks written by Protestants; our text on the Eucharist was written by a British Methodist. That was not in Dallas, by the way—it was on Long Island.

These stories could be multiplied literally ad infinitum. It was and is typical in this country that young men presenting themselves for formation are subjected to situations that undermine their faith and morals. This is not because the seminary is wired for cable TV. It is because the bishops of this country permit it to be so.

The situation was so serious so long ago that in the early 1980s, the Vicar of Christ directed that a visitation of all American seminaries, an unprecedented event, occur. This visitation was entrusted to the bishops of our country. It was carried out while I was still in seminary, and under our bishops it was rendered a toothless joke.

Enough, then, about the corrosive effects of secular culture on seminarians and young priests. The biggest obstacle to their formation as priests after the heart of Jesus is their own fathers in God.

"Church-Bashing" in the Media?

One commentary I read on the situation crossed over the line into the offensive and the harmful when it spoke of the media. I read with disbelief lines such as these: "But, come on; we know what this is really about, don't we? The current feeding frenzy in the press has little to do with any real concern for the victims of sexual abuse.... Throughout this country the haters of the Catholic Church are grinding their axes, ecstatic at the chance." Or this chestnut: "All the indignant cries for justice emanating from the Church-bashers in the media are a sham." Or this: "Their true aim is to hurt the Church, to damage its credibility."

What could we possibly say that is bad enough about such a superficial, shallow analysis?

First off, we must distinguish between factual reporting and opinion/ editorial. Factual reporting we judge on the basis of the comprehensiveness, fairness, and clarity of the reporting of facts. Editorial, being opinion, rises or falls on the strength of the facts on which it is based, the case that is built upon them, and the mode of expression. In my own judgment, for example, the opinion pieces of commentator Jimmy Breslin are skewed, biased, and worthless, although he has the right to express those opinions. But I had better be able to distinguish between such opinion pieces and the reporting of facts.

Friday morning I watched Massachusetts District Attorney Margaret Coakley preside at the press conference on the arrest of Fr. Paul Shanley. She went out of her way to observe that her office lacked the resources to conduct manhunts. She commended the media for using its resources not just to locate Fr. Shanley but to research and profile the activities of predator priests like him so that the authorities and the public understood better the seriousness of the problem. She observed that there were many victims who were experiencing some relief at this arrest, and they have the media to thank for it.

Not the Church. The media.

With a file full, one and a half thousand pages on the disgusting activities of Shanley, two cardinals of the archdiocese of Boston thought he'd make a good pastor. Because of that, starting at the age of six a boy was raped repeatedly for years by his pastor. It was the complaint of that boy, now twenty-four and scarred for life, that landed Shanley in jail. As far as the Church was concerned, he was fit to be a pastor, fit to travel all over the country lecturing, fit to give a lecture as part of my seminary training. Worthy of a warm, glowing letter of commendation from Cardinal Bernard Law as late as 1997.

In this light, I honestly find offensive the remarks about the media in that commentary on the "Church bashers." The writer begins his essay by noting that there are many good priests. Obviously, he is concerned that they not all be tarred with the same brush. How ironic that he then turns and does precisely that to the media. In the media, and in public life, there are people who have performed a signal service to the victims, which their Church was not willing or able to perform, and they performed a service for the Church itself, which quite evidently is in more trouble than it realizes.

The Dallas Case

Take the Dallas case. *None* of the victims of Frs. Rudy Kos, Robert Peebles, or Billy Hughes went first to the media. Nor did they go first to their attorneys. They went to the Church first; there, they were stonewalled, lied to, misled, as delay tactics were used to push the matter past the statute of limitations.

Fr. Peebles was arrested for attempted rape of a boy on the Air Force base where he served as chaplain. The boy, from Peebles' former parish in Dallas, was visiting him for the weekend. The diocese of Dallas prevented his prosecution by arranging for a discharge on condition that he get treatment, as their pastor assured the boy's parents that the priest would get help.

Well, he did not. The diocese broke its promise to the parents of the boy and to the armed forces. Fr. Peebles was reassigned, to St. Augustine Church in Dallas. From there he was arrested for abusing kids—and the people of St. Augustine and the family of the first boy found out that in both instances, Peebles had been assigned to their parishes with prior histories of abusing kids. There was *no warning* to the parishioners at all.

Fr. Bill Hughes carried on an affair nightly with a fifteen-year-old girl until her mom got suspicious and found love letters. She brought them to a trusted priest, who took them and promised to pass them on. It would be dealt with. The letters were never seen again, of course, and nothing was done with Fr. Hughes.

The Fr. Kos case makes no sense from soup to nuts. He was married in the Church and divorced, yet someone wanted him in the seminary so badly that a fraudulent annulment was obtained for him. This *despite* the fact that his wife contacted the diocese to say, "He can't be a *priest!* I threw him out because he likes *boys!*" Someone wanted to keep him so badly that the administration and vicar general ignored the complaints of seminarians—including persons known to me and friends of mine—that Kos, in the seminary, was preying upon the college seminarians.

When the Kos case was done, the judge did an unusual thing. He read, at the request of the jury, a statement from them publicly rebuking the bishop of Dallas and the vicar general for testimony that was obfuscatory and not forthcoming. Again, please remember, the victims did not first go to the press or to the law office. But the press and the law office were their refuge when their Church betrayed them.

And let us not palaver that nonsensical "If we had known then what we know now ..." The terrible effects of clergy sexual abuse on victims and families, and the cretinous harm done by Church stonewalling, was quite clear to us in Dallas from the 1984 Gilbert Gauthe case in Lafayette, Louisiana—we had Lafayette guys studying with us. We *all* knew of the damage done by the vicar general and bishop there. Just as the Boston folk knew of Dallas.

Enough *Mea Culpas?*

One of my problems with the essay I read is that the writer produced a brief cheerleading piece on an immensely complicated subject that requires nuanced care instead. Let me give you an example from my experience that made me cringe when I read in that essay this strident statement: "For goodness sakes, enough with the *mea culpas!*"

A lady named Janet Patterson lives with her husband in the diocese of Wichita, Kansas. They have raised their family to be devout Catholics. Her son Eric, a remarkably gifted young man who had a lot of accomplishments to his credit, killed himself perhaps two years ago at the age of twenty-nine. Shortly before that, the family had discovered that the reason for the deep depression that plagued Eric was the sexual abuse he had suffered at the hands of his parish priest as an altar boy, from the age of thirteen.

Janet, who is a teacher, went to the diocese to tell them about the abuse her son had suffered at the hands of Fr. Larson. The priest she spoke with in the chancery office was well known to her—he had grown up in her town. He listened to her and grew very still and sad. He told her, "We had no idea this went back to then. Father Larson is no longer serving as a priest. We thought the abuse started in the parish after yours."

Janet left somewhat comforted. At least she had the consolation of knowing that her diocese had not knowingly put this predator, who was responsible for her son's death, in their parish.

Then, of course, she found out that it wasn't true. Fr. Larson had indeed abused kids in the parishes before hers and had been moved around like a chess piece. It would be nice to think that it is at least theoretically possible for chancery officials to tell the truth once in a while, but evidently this is not a consolation we are granted in this life.

Six altar boys who had served under this priest committed suicide.

Fr. Larson is in jail today—but not thanks to the Church. As for Janet and her family, they live with a deep sense of estrangement from the Church they loved, a Church that had once been such a part of their family life.

"We Did Not Know"?

I was put in touch with the Pattersons through the editor of the Catholic newspaper *The Wanderer,* and we have spoken often. I asked Fr. Tom Doyle, O.P., who was at the time stationed in the Midwest, to give Janet a call. He said, "But she's just three states away"—and he *drove* there.

Do you know of Fr. Doyle? He was once the secretary to the papal pro nuncio in Washington. He helped develop the 1985 secret report on the potential ramifications of the pedophilia crisis. He produced a report predicting a staggering array of scandals, billions of dollars in legal fees, and more.

The report was shelved by the bishops. So was Fr. Doyle, who pressed for the report's acceptance and was canned. He has been in an ecclesial limbo since but has made himself helpful to the victims and their attorneys as they come up in litigation against bishops like Cardinal Law. These latter perpetually bleat, "But we did not know!" about things that were in Fr. Doyle's report to them seventeen years ago.

I wish I could say, "So that's the story," but it isn't even the beginning of the story. It is a tiny sliver—a tiny sliver of a huge, sordid, perverted epic.

I believe that the writer of the commentary I read wants to be strongly supportive of the Church and the priesthood and wants to encourage others to do the same. Unfortunately, I believe that the unintended effect of an essay like his will be precisely the opposite; it was certainly not an encouragement to me as a priest. In fact, it was utterly demoralizing.

We cannot look at this pedophilia scandal in isolation. There are at least twelve *major areas* of the life of our Church that are in serious crisis—and have been for two generations. I think of liturgy, catechesis, scriptural scholarship, moral theology, religious life, seminaries, the priesthood, marriage, and family life, for starters.

I think of the faithful lay Catholics who have striven insistently to bring to the attention of the bishops and the Holy See the crises of our Church. I think of how often it could have been the case that our bishops might have helped and healed, if only they were capable of responding as human beings to people in pain. The whole country has been appalled at how they have not "gotten it," at how utterly divorced from the ordinary concerns of people the bishops have been. (If you think this is overstating the case, think of Paul Shanley roaming the country and of the number of bishops who made that possible, in Boston and elsewhere, before you draw your final conclusion.)

No. We have not had *enough* of the *mea culpas*. I do not think Janet Patterson has heard all that she needs to from the bishop who has never been in touch with her, let alone from the Cardinal of Boston, who thinks Shanley was an example of "poor record keeping." As though, if the Boston chancery improves its secretarial skills, there will be no pedophiles left in the archdiocese. As though two cardinals needed help figuring out what Margaret Gallant, a laywoman, knew and told them about John Geoghan: that he did not need to be a priest.

No. We do not need to blame MTV and sexually explicit media for things we have fostered in our own institutions.

No. We should be embarrassed and ashamed to blame the media for "Church-bashing" when they are just pointing out the sordid facts about how our bishops go about their business. If society were indifferent to the fact that there are pedophile priests, and bishops who cover up for them, *then* we would have reason to be outraged. We have *no reason* to be outraged that they take our teachings in this area more seriously than we do. We have *no reason* to be outraged at them because they are outraged that we do not live up to our own teachings.

The Real Enemies of the Faith

As a priest, I find it demoralizing and outrageous that someone would issue a call to arms to faithful Catholic groups such as the Knights of Malta, the Knights of Columbus, the Catholic League, and others, to go into battle against the very people who, as far as I can see, have done us a great service. They have pointed out the real enemies of the faith.

The real enemies of the faith are *not* the attorneys, the reporters covering the stories, the pundits weighing in. Indeed, even Jimmy Breslin, much as I personally dislike his punditry, can't be counted as the real enemy. He's bush league compared to the real enemy—the enemy within. This enemy's failure to oversee and govern, to guide and rebuke and foster the good, has permitted dissenters over two generations, within the house of God, to teach under Catholic auspices, preach with faculties, and undermine the Catholic faith and liturgy; to administer seminaries in which every kind of aberration was tolerated; to bring things to a point where the Catholic father of his family has to fret over whether his son can be an altar boy, whether his children can be entrusted to the diocesan catechetical program.

We have seen the enemy. It ain't MTV. If someone wants to mobilize the Knights of Malta and the Knights of Columbus, let's have a crusade demanding of the bishops solid catechetics, sound liturgy in the Roman tradition, an end to the situation in which, when we encounter a teacher under Catholic auspices—whether in a parish school, CCD program, college, university, seminary diocesan workshop, whatever—we have to figure out whether or not this person is, not just an orthodox Catholic, but a Christian.

Focus on the enemy. The enemy is within. As a parish priest I am telling you: MTV doesn't undermine my ministry as much as the enemy within.

Don't bother jousting with MTV. Stop. Think. Realize that the Church is in crisis and has been for two generations. That there are folk who have the authority to address that but, instead of doing so, have allowed the Church to become a possibly unsafe place for your kids.

Ask yourself who the real enemy is. I don't think you'll finally focus on Britney Spears.

❖

Fr. Joseph F. Wilson is a priest of the diocese of Brooklyn and a frequent contributor to several Catholic publications.

THREE

A Moment of Grace for the Church
The Dynamic Renewal of Seminary Culture

Mark Lowery

If there ever was a time to solve a crisis by getting to its root causes, this is it. To get to the root causes of the current sexual abuse scandals in the Church, we first have to identify the crisis properly. It is not a crisis about pedophilia, a rare phenomenon is which prepubescent children are abused, either homosexually or heterosexually.[1] The crisis is about a few priests of homosexual inclination who have committed criminal acts by seducing adolescent boys (not *pedophilia*, but *ephebophilia*) and whose acts have been covered up.

The root cause, then, is *(a)* the approval of homosexual behavior in the culture at large, and the existence of a gay subculture, which *(b)* has found its way into the Church, where there is now a microcosm of that gay subculture. This subculture has developed not because most leaders support it but because a few leaders who tolerate it have gained an upper hand.[2]

A Renewal of Seminary Formation: Participated Theonomy

It is, counterintuitively, a moment of grace for the Church. Just as the events of 9/11 allowed us to see reality in stark clarity, so too the ephebophiliac crisis allows us to see with frightening clarity a condition within the Church that has, till now, been swept under the carpet. That condition is the existence of a flawed program of moral and spiritual formation in place at some seminaries, a program that allows an *autonomous* view of morality, in which the individual ends up as the ultimate arbiter over what is right and what is wrong.

The solution—one of John Paul II's key directives to the American episcopate—is a genuine renewal of seminary education and formation. With a renewed program, there will no longer be a magnet within some seminaries to attract sincere but misled people who are part of the gay subculture.

Let us first consider what that renewed program looks like. The good news is that it is already alive and well in numerous seminaries and other organs of Catholic education.

The antidote to the autonomous method that has crept into some seminaries is not a simplistic return to an emphasis on moral rules, an approach used in the moral manuals of the past. In his encyclical *Veritatis Splendor* (hereafter referred to as *VS*)[3] the Pope calls such an approach a *heteronomy*—a situation in which moral rules are extrinsically imposed, unconnected to the person—and it is every bit as problematic as *autonomy*. It was precisely too heteronomous an approach that in part caused the wild swing toward autonomy, so let us avoid another wild swing back to a mere set of legalisms.

The proper approach lies within the perspective the Pope calls *participated theonomy*. Participated theonomy is an approach to the moral life in which the truth—which includes absolute moral norms—is presented as truly fulfilling of the deepest needs of the person. One of its essential features is that the challenges of the moral life are placed within the theological context of *(a)* a life of virtuous habits, that are *(b)* developed as an intrinsic component of a rich spiritual life that allows the full power of Christ's grace. As *Veritatis Splendor* notes, Christ "has set our freedom free from the domination of concupiscence."[4] Participated theonomy is essential not just for seminary education but for all of Catholic education, from CCD classes to the high school and then the college religion curriculum. Again, the current crisis is a wake-up call for educators, pastors, and administrators at every level.

Veritatis Splendor is the charter for developing a framework, a "culture," of participated theonomy. It shows how an array of revisionist methodologies have led not to a newfound freedom but to slavery, slavery to the passions. Consider, for example, two moral theories decried in *VS:* "proportionalism" and the "fundamental option theory." Proportionalism allows a person to consider personal circumstances and intentions before determining whether an act is intrinsically evil. A misused fundamental option theory emphasizes that grave sins need not be mortal sins so long as one's fundamental attitude is not one that despises God.

How Relativism Works Its Damage

Imagine this scenario. Seminarians are studying the topic of moral norms in their course on moral theology. They come in knowing that the moral norms of the Church have an absolute character to them—the Ten Commandments are not the Ten Suggestions. And in fact their professor affirms these moral norms, but he affirms them as *ideals.* He notes that everyone should always strive to follow them—as ideals they are not negotiable. An all-out relativism is to be avoided at all costs.

Next on the syllabus is the topic "rare exceptions." Because of the sheer complexity of life, the professor says, there are rare situations in which one may justifiably fall short of a particular high ideal. One must be very cautious here, follow one's conscience, and be sure that a genuine love of God is at the core of one's being (a "fundamental option" toward God). But with those caveats, one can make, very rarely, exceptions to moral norms contingent on the circumstances and intentions of the agent.

The professor has no intention whatsoever of setting the stage for a relativistic moral free-for-all. The motive, rather, is pastoral compassion for those in truly challenging situations. But there's the rub: The very nature of our moral lives is that we find ourselves in challenging moral quandaries, situations in which we come up against a solid moral norm and wonder, "Might my case be the rare exception to this absolute principle?" Or put a bit less academically, "There's a good rule out there, but I might have to break it."

That is a prime instance of the concupiscent tendency at work. When the professor presents a system that allows rare exceptions, he places the seminarians on a dangerous trajectory. Unfortunately, those who conclude that they themselves constitute the rare exception are not rare!

These moral theories are much more complex than so quick a summary suggests, and they actually raise important questions about the moral tradition that need to be addressed. But in the hands of young people in priestly formation, they open up a Pandora's box that redounds to an *autonomous* view of the moral life, that view, as we noted, which holds the individual to be the arbiter over what is right and what is wrong. The encyclical *Veritatis Splendor* examines a half dozen or so popular theories and finds that they, often inadvertently, lead right down the path of moral autonomy. Without intending relativism, they nonetheless set the stage for it—the concupiscent tendency takes care of the rest, and the surrounding culture certainly does nothing to help.

The New "Theology of the Body"

As we have noted, the antidote to such autonomy is not a blind, self-indulgent return to heteronomous legalisms. Absolute moral norms are essential, but they must be cast within the fresh perspective of participated theonomy. There the norms are in the service of the genuine fulfillment of the person, placed in the context of a life of virtue and a deep spiritual life. The moral norms that concern sexuality are, of course, of special interest here.

Now for the really good news essential to this moment of grace in the Church: We have right in our midst a remarkable way to learn about and live the truth about sexuality in the perspective of participated theonomy. It is called the *theology of the body,* an approach spearheaded by the Pope himself[5] and being disseminated industriously and creatively by a variety of theologians.

There is a powerful sexual dynamism in our sexuality, what we often call the sexual urge. The current crisis is fundamentally a diabolic instance of that dynamism misused and gone awry, and secondarily a question of mismanagement (the cover-up). The serious attention that the management problem deserves must not obscure the deeper problem and its solution: placing this powerful sexual dynamism within the *theology of the body.* In the seminarian's formation in the theology of the body, he learns that the body is not something upon which he can impose his own meanings, but it has its own transcendent meanings awaiting his discovery.

"The person ... discovers in the body the anticipatory signs, the expression and the promise of the gift of self," says John Paul, "in conformity with the wise plan of the creator" (*VS*, 48). Hence, the body "speaks a language," a language of anticipatory signs, providing parameters within which we live the moral life. It is not as if the body were mere raw material "out there," over and against us, upon which we exercise our moral decisions. Rather, the body is integral to us as persons, and its language contributes to those decisions. The body provides "rational indicators," "reference points," or "anticipatory signs" that require reason and free will.

Here we are at the heart of participated theonomy: The individual person has the personal responsibility to grasp or "mine" the meaning of the body and then freely to align him or herself with the meaning. Then the transcendent truth that the Creator has infused into the body is not a heteronomous imposition but rather something that each person participates in: The truth is carried in each person's own body, and each person freely grasps and lives that truth, making it his or her own.

What is the language the body speaks? The powerful sexual dynamism of the body—the sexual urge—is to be used in a *self-giving* way that treats others as persons, not as objects. For married people, treating the spouse as a person, not a mere sexual object, requires fidelity and a full respect for that place in the marital adventure where God might create new life: the sacred interplay of female fertility and the conjugal act. Otherwise put, it requires a full, *pure* respect for the unitive and procreative meanings of conjugal love.

For the celibate person, the sexual dynamism of the body is not repressed but is channeled in another direction: a total, faithful giving of self to God and the Christian community. Celibacy, properly understood and lived, is thus the solution to the current crisis, not part of the problem.

When the language of self-gift is ignored, when individuals impose their own meaning on the dynamism of the body—a meaning not from the Creator but a meaning that takes its cue from the individual's own concupiscent tendency—then the crisis begins. For the ephebophiliac homosexual priest, it is a horrid phenomenon. The priest convinces himself that, given his challenging condition, he is an exception to the moral norms about sexuality—and he gets at least a nod from the proportionalist method he learned regarding absolute moral norms.

In addition, the widespread use of contraceptives by otherwise good (but perhaps invincibly ignorant) Catholic couples has created a climate of autonomy with regard to sexual mores that allows him to forge his own meaning for the body. After all, if married couples can disjoin the unitive and procreative meanings of the body, why should he not so manipulate them? He convinces his victim that they have a secret relationship that will be just fine so long as it is kept secret.

In doing so, he has entirely ignored the transcendent meaning of the body and imposed his own selfish meaning onto it. And he has convinced himself and his seduced victim that this pure selfishness is their own special private way of self-giving. This is the precise opposite of the true meaning of the language of the body—a perverse instance of *lying* with the body rather than speaking truthfully with it.

The Impact of Purity

Once the Church responds—pray God—to this moment of grace and infuses seminary education with participated theonomy, there will be no more "magnetic draw" into some seminaries from the gay culture. When it comes to admitting young men to the seminary, pastors well grounded in this approach will be able to discern whether a young man is on the right trajectory of moral and spiritual growth and development. The Church must not admit candidates who are not solidly on the pathway of being absolutely pure persons, and those in charge of priestly formation must be well along on that path as well.

The *Catechism of the Catholic Church* teaches about a threefold purity. The pure of heart are "those who have attuned their intellects and wills to the demands of God's holiness, chiefly in three areas: charity; chastity or sexual rectitude; love of truth and orthodoxy of faith."[6] As Deal Hudson notes:

> A priestly vocation, like a marriage, requires the mutual and free consent of both parties. Thus, the Church must discern that a candidate is indeed worthy and fit mentally, physically, and spiritually to commit to a life of priestly service. A candidate's desire for the priesthood does not constitute a vocation in and of itself. Spiritual and vocation directors are now even more attuned to the character flaws that would make an otherwise qualified man an unfit candidate.[7]

An important and much debated issue emerges here: Is the homosexual inclination *ipso facto* one such disqualifying character flaw? To answer that question, a critical distinction is in order.

Recall St. Paul's thankfulness to God for giving him a "thorn in his flesh" (see 2 Cor 12:7) that made him constantly aware of his utter dependence on God. We all live the moral life in the context of damaged "raw material." We all have our respective crosses to bear— we all suffer from the primal disorder of concupiscence—and we all have the capacity to do as we ought, particularly with the grace of Christ. A heterosexual seminarian will have to work consistently to live his celibate calling, and the threefold purity, nurtured on the trajectory of participated theonomy, will make his chaste living *habitual.*

A person of homosexual orientation has an added burden: He must struggle with concupiscence, as the heterosexual does, but in the context of a sexual disorder. If we really take seriously the Church's teaching on homosexuality, we must believe invariably that all homosexual persons are called to be celibate (with the exception of successful instances of reparative therapy), and we must simultaneously hold that with Christ's grace these persons *can* live the chaste lives they *ought* to live.

The Congregation for the Doctrine of the Faith has observed: "What is at all costs to be avoided is the unfounded and demeaning assumption that the sexual behavior of homosexual persons is always and totally compulsive and therefore inculpable." [8] In some cases, perhaps rare ones, chaste living can be so *habitual* that the individual can move through seminary formation and into the priesthood with the homosexual disorder in virtually complete abeyance.

The fact is, many homosexual persons are far from that trajectory of habitual chastity, just as are many heterosexuals. They might engage in numerous chaste acts, out of sheer conviction and willpower, but without the *habit,* they walk a thin line. It would be blatantly unfair— a "near occasion of sin," a "setup"—to ask such an individual to go through seminary training, as unfair as it would be to have a young heterosexual male live in a community of young women with all activities held in common. It would be unfair to invite such young men into seminary formation, just as it would be unfair to invite many heterosexuals whose sexual urge is not habituated chastely. Prudence must dictate.

It is always tempting to take what is *often* the prudent path (disallowing admission, reporting an impropriety to proper authorities) and make it into an absolute whereby that path is required in every instance. While looking to be a firm, decisive move, it instead shifts the focus away from the larger issue: the renewal of seminary formation.

Now is the moment for that renewal, already well underway in many places. Perhaps this can be one of the great (and one of the final?) acts of John Paul II: a concretization of his theology of the body and his great encyclical *Veritatis Splendor*. Such an achievement would require an efficacious command to remove from seminaries any who teach or allow erroneous views of the Church's moral norms, followed by the installation of holy leaders. Steering a course between autonomy and heteronomy, they would foster an atmosphere attractive to young men devoted to Christ and the Church and conducive to the development of the threefold purity of orthodoxy, chastity, and charity.

:✦:

Mark Lowery, Ph.D., is associate professor of moral theology at the University of Dallas and a columnist for Envoy *Magazine.*

1. See Deal Hudson, "11 Myths About the Priestly Pedophilia Controversy," www.crisismagazine.com/freeletter.htm.

2. See the important essay by Rev. Paul Shaughnessy, "The Gay Priest Problem," *Catholic World Report*, May 2002, 44-51.

3. John Paul II, *Veritatis Splendor* (1993). Hereafter cited as *VS*.

4. *VS*, note 104.

5. The Pope's homilies at his Wednesday audiences are collected in *The Theology of the Body: Human Love in the Divine Plan* (Boston: Pauline, 1993).

6. *CCC* 2518; 1 Tm 4: 3-9; 2 Tm 2:22; 1 Thes 4:7; Col 3:5; Eph 4:19; Ti 1:15; 1 Tm 1:3-4; 2 Tm 2:23-26.

7. Hudson, point 11.

8. Congregation for the Doctrine of the Faith, "And the Truth Will Make You Free: Letter to Bishops of the Catholic Church on the Pastoral Care of Homosexual Persons," art. 11.

FOUR

Something Good Is Coming
The Great Awakening Ahead

Michael Novak

On a fairly regular basis, the Lord makes his people suffer, his Church, his Beloved. The present has been such a time, and our own sins have brought on our troubles. The much acclaimed "Church of Vatican II," the church of "the progressives," energized since 1965 by dissent and rebellion against many traditions and teachings of the Church, and intent upon foisting on the Church a new morality of sex and marriage and birth and priesthood, has made an awful botch of things.

In 1964 I called my first book *A New Generation: American and Catholic.* Magazines in those days were full of stories about "the New Breed" of priests and laity and how great the "renewed" church would be. Implicitly, how much better than the old.

We certainly showed them. Never has the Catholic Church in America been so shamed, humiliated, and mortified before the whole world. The "new morality" of the New Breed has turned into a disgrace.

Much good, of course, has been done in and through the Church during the last forty years. Many things—ecumenism, for instance— have been made better. (In my opinion, the liturgy in many ways is far worse done than earlier, with far less respect and far less sense of holiness, dignity, and awe.) Openness and dialogue are much better, even though some have taken "openness" to mean an inner hollowness, without content or character of its own.

The current scandals, alas, have made the name "Catholic" a badge of self-inflicted shame, a shame inflicted by a tiny proportion of the clergy.

The "Progressive" Dream

If interviews in the press are correct, some of these culprits actually picture themselves as an advance party for a new and better sexual morality than that of the tradition they loathe. They are not in favor of celibacy—and certainly not of chastity, either—but of "self-exploration" and "self-acceptance of one's own body and its pleasures," of "being at home in one's own body," and other such rationalizations.

To some extent, this pattern may be explained by the tsunami of the sexual revolution of the sixties and seventies, that earthquake, hurricane, tidal wave which threw millions of souls into confusion about who and what to believe about authentic morality. Many good people, conservative as well as liberal, were thrown off balance in those days. A fairly large proportion of Catholics, like others, may be tempted to rationalize their own errors of those days, by trying now to "normalize" what in other ages was taken as plainly sinful or, to use the current secular term, "deviant" behavior. Abortion, for instance, adultery, homosexual actions.

But the sexual revolution does not explain the full pride of the "reformers" of Vatican II who, when the ink was not yet dry on the decrees of that council, were already foreseeing Vatican III and a wholly new church of their imagination.

A utopian church of the progressive dream emerged, always different from the Church dragged down by the weight of the actual Rome of Pope Paul VI (in his day as loathed by progressives as John Paul II is today). In the name of this airy and future church, all sorts of opinions and actions and policies were countenanced as "forward-looking" that in other ages would have been seen as wanderings far from authentic faith.

This was the climate within which the "deviancy" that brought on the current scandals prospered, undetected, undeterred. Note, for instance, that most of the scandals being reported in 2002 actually happened more than ten years ago, in the heyday of those thirty most progressive years from 1965 until about 1993. About that time, reforms instituted by the bishops began to take effect. Many badly errant seminaries were cleaned out or shut down. A number of new, more orthodox and traditional seminaries began to bear good fruit and to prosper in vocations.

The change already under way in many places is tangible.

Nurturing the Chaste Life

The life of celibacy can be a very hard one, especially in times of aridity in prayer, and career frustration, and normal loneliness—and when acute temptations arise in situations almost wholly undefended by safeguards and precautions, by ascetical practices, and by a surrounding community of loving fidelity and chastity. Maintaining chastity requires abundant graces. These require silence and prayer for their reception.

A life too long lived apart from intense daily prayer, meditation on the lives of the saints, the devout praying of the Daily Office of the Church, and a slowly and reflectively enacted sacrifice of the Mass each day is not a life in which the probabilities of fidelity are enhanced. On the contrary, the probabilities of chastity decline exponentially, as neglect of the life of the spirit extends its control, like a summer drought spreading its reach across sun-baked fields. Where the love of God withers, the love of this world gains a chokehold.

There is a lesson in the present time: The prayerful, orthodox, and faithful priests and religious of this generation did not bring about the scandals that now humiliate the Church. The sins that have brought us low were abetted by a culture of rebellion, pride, and moral superiority among those who thought themselves more intelligent, more able, more in tune with human progress, open, experimental, and brave. They despised the merely traditional, observant, and orthodox, whom they considered closed-minded, rigid, and intransigent.

They turned away from the tried and true asceticism and paths of holiness of the past. The sins that have disgraced us are the sins of those who promised "renewal" and "progress" down "new" paths.

"But we did not mean child abuse," the progressives will say in self-defense. "We didn't mean the abuse of teenagers."

But, hey, a climate in which it was regarded as "rigid" to say that sex outside of marriage was sinful was not a climate in which playground sand long held lines drawn in it. Young people in premarital coupling, older couples "experimenting" beyond the marriage bond, and same-sex coupling were in that climate not regarded as "disordered" but as "healthy experimentation."

"When is the Catholic Church ever going to get over its Victorian moral qualms and get up-to-date with contemporary sex science?" was the subject of many a dinner-party interlude. Remember those days?

An Error of Anthropology

The "progressive" vision of the human being embodies a profound error of anthropology. It imagines human beings to be "persons" whose bodies are somehow separable from these genderless "persons" and malleable for deployment in any of a number of culturally and personally preferential ways, so long as the person of the other is "respected" and, in its fashion, "loved."

Progressivism, in short, is a form of gnosticism. Its systematic separation of body and person (soul) is a very ancient heresy. The moral dissoluteness to which it gradually leads has been witnessed in many earlier cycles of human history.

For the curing of this disease, the greatest kindness is strict adherence to a more demanding regimen: respect for a more accurate anthropology of the embodied person, the spirited body, the incarnate person, the flesh-and-blood human being fashioned by the Creator for his own inhabitation. This is the regimen of the oneness and wholeness of God's transcendent love, diffused by understanding, reflection, and loving choice through every organ, member, and fiber of human tissue. It is the regimen of that chastity of the heart that is, to paraphrase Kierkegaard, to will one love.

The current humiliation of the Catholic Church will, I feel sure, lead to the great grace of remembrance—remembrance of our true and most precious inheritance, trust in the Word of God bequeathed to us by the ancient Church and by the Sacred Scripture to whose canonical status it attests.

"He is no Catholic who is not united in *sacra doctrina* [sacred doctrine] with the bishop of Rome," Stanislaus Hosius says, on a tablet memorialized on the walls of S. Maria in Trastevere in Rome, the titular church of the great Cardinal James Gibbons.

A Great Awakening

There is coming an awakening of a great love for orthodoxy, for fidelity, for clinging to the whole truth as it was handed down to us. There is also arising, justifiably, a certain hard-won contempt for the learned doctors whose pride led them to try to sell us a bill of goods for, lo, so many decades now. To what a miserable state have they reduced their lower regions of the Church.

The good and solid things of the Tradition have proved more reliable than they. By far.

These are the notes I look to hear from Rome, more sweetly said, during the coming weeks and months—and maybe days.

Michael Novak, the George F. Jewett scholar at the American Enterprise Institute, is the author, most recently, of On Two Wings: Humble Faith and Common Sense at the American Founding. *This article is copyright 2002 by Michael Novak and first appeared in the April 23, 2002, edition of* National Review Online *(www.nationalreview.com). Used with permission.*

FIVE

Is Celibacy to Blame?
Separating Fact From Fiction

Raymond Arroyo

L isten to the chatter surrounding the priestly sex abuse scandals, and you would imagine that every cassock conceals a child predator—or at least a pervert. By magnifying a tiny minority of priestly offenders, some in the media have us believing that all priests are pedophiles, though the evidence suggests otherwise.

Once that splendidly alliterative term "pedophile priest" traveled through the pop culture, (the majority of) good clerics were convicted with the bad. Judgment pronounced, a media remedy was needed—an explanation for this aberrant behavior. If priests are the preeminent pedophiles in society, there must be some shared attribute driving them to abuse our children.

Perhaps their collars are cutting off the air supply to the brain, causing a strange psychosexual imbalance. Maybe the daily consumption of altar wine over time chemically excites the sex drive. Nah, ridiculous, you say? But no more ridiculous than the answer some reporters and pundits arrived at.

"Celibacy is the cause," they said. "Celibacy has driven these priests to violate the young! Forget personal sin or evil—celibacy is to blame! So if you want to protect our children," the line goes, "give priests the freedom to have sex and plenty of it." Hmmm.

The Stats Show Otherwise

When he met with the U.S. cardinals to formulate a response to the horrific scandals besieging the Church, the Pope took the issue of clerical celibacy off the table as a cure-all. Against the strident voices of dissenters, disaffected clergy, the media, and at least one American cardinal, His Holiness suggested that celibacy was part of the solution, not the problem. And the facts seem to bear him out.

In 1992 the archdiocese of Chicago reviewed some 2,252 priest personnel files. They found that only forty priests—1.8 percent—had been guilty of sexual misconduct at some point in their career. Of that forty, only one was a pedophile.

Another study by Penn State Professor Philip Jenkins reveals that a mere 0.3 percent of priests are pedophiles. Married men abuse children in far greater numbers. Anywhere from 3 to 8 percent, if you believe the studies.

So statistically, children are far safer with the celibates. As the U.S. cardinals said in their report of April 24: "A link between celibacy and pedophilia cannot be scientifically maintained." So much for the group think.

"But if only these men had a spouse, a sexual outlet, they would not need to turn to kids," goes the conventional wisdom (and the screeds regularly littering the op-ed pages). Aside from reducing women to little more than child protection devices, there are logical holes here.

Putting aside the media fixation with the Catholic Church, it is important to point out, as the *Christian Science Monitor* recently did, that the majority of sexual abuse allegations in America occur in Protestant churches. There are thirty-five hundred sex abuse allegations a year—roughly seventy a week in Protestant churches, according to the Christian Ministry Resource Survey. Remember, these are churches where *married* clergy and volunteers predominate. If the objective is to stop the abuse before us and prohibit its happening again, the Protestant statistics prove that marriage is no insurance policy.

Since the victims in 98 percent of the alleged Catholic abuse cases were teenage boys, allowing priests to marry (women) seems a pointless solution. There is just no correlation between the offense and the corrective. You may as well offer the alcoholic priest the deed to a dairy and call him cured.

The Real Cause: Lack of Celibacy

If the truth be known: These scandals were not caused by celibacy. These scandals were caused by a lack of celibacy. The ancient discipline has gotten a bad rap in the chaos of the last few months. Celibacy was never an arbitrary penance for Catholic ministers but a sacrifice so they might, in the words of Pope Paul VI, "acquire a deeper mastery of soul and body and a fuller maturity (to) more perfectly receive the blessedness spoken of in the gospel."

The Church's discipline is intended to draw men and women to greater depths of holiness, weakening and diminishing the power of the flesh. According to Catholic teaching, this discipline purifies the individual and expands his or her ability to love. Msgr. Lorenzo Albecete explains celibacy this way: "It is the radical, outward expression of the poverty of the human heart, the poverty that makes true love possible by preventing it from corrupting into possession or manipulation." Recent opinion columns would have us believe the exact opposite.

The roots of celibacy are also deeply misunderstood by the pop culture. According to the folks on TV, celibacy was something "imposed on the priesthood" during the Middle Ages to keep the children of clerics from inheriting Church property. (If only I could receive an out-of-court settlement for every time I've heard this.) Actually, the real history is far more interesting, and complex.

To begin with, Christ himself was a celibate, so it is no surprise that the early Church and the Scripture itself salutes and commends the practice. In Matthew's Gospel, Christ lauds those who "have made themselves eunuchs for the sake of the kingdom of heaven" (Mt 19:12). In his First Letter to the Corinthians, St. Paul, another celibate, writes: "The unmarried man is anxious about the affairs of the Lord,... but the married man is anxious about worldly affairs, how to please his wife, and his interests are divided" (1 Cor 7:32-34).

From the time of Christ forward, celibacy was the Catholic norm for priests—married clergy were merely tolerated. According to pious tradition, even married apostles, such as St. Peter, left their wives (with their permission) to undertake their ministry as celibates. Whatever the case, there is little doubt where the Church officially stood on the matter by the fourth century. In 385 Pope Siricius issued the first papal decree on priestly celibacy. He said, "All of us who are priests are bound by a strict law to dedicate both body and heart to sobriety and chastity by virtue of our ordination."

Five years later the Council of Carthage announced: "Previous councils have decreed that bishops, priests, and deacons must be continent and perfectly chaste, as becomes ministers of God ... as the Apostles taught." By the Council of Toledo in 633, a bishop's permission was needed for a priest to marry. Finally, in 1139, Pope Gregory VII declared celibacy mandatory for all priests, formalizing in law what had been the general practice for centuries.

The canard that the papacy imposed the rule of celibacy to protect Church properties from greedy spouses and offspring is simply not true (no matter how often it is repeated on Oprah). But there is a spiritual explanation. Starting in the third century, married priests were required to abstain from sex the night before offering Mass. The notion was this: Separate yourselves from the worldly, and focus on the transcendent. As the demand for the sacraments increased, these men were abstaining from sex continuously. Thus, like all things in the Church, a practice rooted in tradition evolved over time and eventually was codified into law.

A People Set Apart

At a time when the world is transfixed by the deviant, where all mysteries are laid bare, these celibate men and women are a contradiction: a people set apart, people who have saved the most precious part of themselves for God alone. People such as Mother Teresa, John Paul II, Mother Angelica, Padre Pio, and countless others have embraced this discipline and demonstrated its power. This dark hour is not the time to cast it away.

When evil is on a rampage, it is lunatic to abandon the holy.

We are right to condemn, and bring to justice, those non-celibate clergymen guilty of these heinous crimes—and those who abused their power to protect them. But let us spare an innocent practice and not strike those who faithfully observe their vows to God, clinging to this holy and well-trod path of sacrifice.

✦

Raymond Arroyo is news director for Eternal Word Television Network (EWTN) and host of "The World Over Live," seen in some seventy million homes each week. He writes from New Orleans. This essay is an expanded version of an article that first appeared in National Review Online *(www.nationalreview.com). Used with permission.*

SIX

The Gay Question
An Issue That Cannot Be Ignored

Rod Dreher

The first thing to understand about the Catholic Church's pedophilia scandal is that it is not technically a pedophilia scandal. Despite the gruesome example of defrocked Boston priest John Geoghan, whose case started the current tidal wave of revelations, the overwhelming majority of priests who have molested minors are not pedophiles—that is, like Geoghan, among the rare adults sexually attracted to prepubescent children. They are, rather, "ephebophiles"—adults who are sexually attracted to postpubescent youths, generally aged twelve to seventeen. And their victims have been almost exclusively boys.

Stephen Rubino, a New Jersey lawyer, says that of the over three hundred alleged victims of priest sex abuse he has represented, roughly 85 percent are boys and were teenagers when the abuse occurred. Dr. Richard Fitzgibbons, an eminent Catholic psychiatrist who has treated scores of victims and priest-perpetrators, says 90 percent of his patients were either teen male victims of priests or priests who abused teen boys.

"Why are 90 percent to 95 percent, and some estimates say as high as 98 percent, of the victims of clergy [abuse] teenage boys?... We need to ask that question, and I think there's a certain reluctance to raise that issue," said the Rev. Donald B. Cozzens, author of *The Changing Face of the Priesthood,* on a recent broadcast of *Meet the Press.*

The reluctance arises, no doubt, partly out of a fear of antagonizing homosexual anti-defamation groups, who resent the stereotype of male homosexuals as pederasts. It's much safer to focus inquiry on the question of mandatory celibacy or the issue of ordaining women. Yet it defies common sense to imagine that an ordinary man, having made a vow not to marry, is therefore going to be sexually attracted to boys.

Indeed, suppose the Second Vatican Council in the 1960s had admitted married men to the ranks of the Catholic priesthood: Would a single adolescent boy molested over the past forty years have escaped his fate? Similarly, if women had been ordained, would that somehow have made sexually predatory gay priests disappear?

A Risky Issue to Raise

No—this is chiefly a scandal about unchaste or criminal homosexuals in the Catholic priesthood, and about far too many in Church leadership who are disinclined to deal with the problem—or worse, who may in some cases be actively involved in the misconduct. For Catholics, to start asking questions about homosexuality in the priesthood is to risk finding out more than many Church members prefer to know. For journalists, to confront the issue is to risk touching the electrified third rail of American popular culture: the dark side of homosexuality. Yet when we learn that the greatest crisis the Catholic Church in America has ever faced has been brought upon it almost wholly by male clerics seducing boys, attention must be paid to the man behind the curtain.

It is true that a great many gay people are sickened and appalled by what these wicked priests have done to boys. Some with a public voice, such as journalist Andrew Sullivan, have vigorously denounced it. At the same time, Sullivan has strongly supported the ministry of gay priests.

How many gay priests are there? No one can say with certainty; the American bishops have never formally studied the issue, and, for obvious reasons, it is all but impossible to determine an accurate number. Richard Sipe, a laicized priest and psychotherapist who has studied the phenomenon of priests and sex abuse for most of his forty-year career, believes 20 percent of Catholic priests are homosexual and that half of those are sexually active. In his book Fr. Cozzens cites various studies putting the total much higher, but these surveys typically suffer from methodological problems that skew the numbers upward.

Yet those who lowball the numbers could equally be accused of wanting to downplay the problem. The Rev. C. John McCloskey, a member of the conservative Opus Dei organization, claimed recently that the number of gay priests is "2 percent to 4 percent at a maximum," or equivalent to the estimated number of homosexuals in the general population. If that were true, however, it would be hard to explain why, according to experts, Catholic priests are dying of AIDS at a higher rate than males in the general population.

The Lavender Mafia

The raw numbers are less important, though, if homosexual priests occupy positions of influence in the vast Catholic bureaucracy; and there seems little doubt that this is the case in the American Church.

Lest this be dismissed as right-wing paranoia, it bears noting that psychotherapist Sipe is no conservative—indeed, he is disliked by many on the Catholic right for his vigorous dissent from Church teaching on sexual morality—yet he is convinced that the sexual abuse of minors is facilitated by a secret, powerful network of gay priests. Sipe has a great deal of clinical and research experience in this field; he has reviewed thousands of case histories of sexually active priests and abuse victims. He is convinced of the existence of what the Rev. Andrew Greeley, the left-wing clerical gadfly, has called a "lavender Mafia."

"This is a system. This is a whole community. You have many good people covering it up," Sipe says. "There is a network of power. A lot of seminary rectors and teachers are part of it, and they move to chancery-office positions, and on to bishoprics. It's part of the ladder of success. It breaks your heart to see the people who suffer because of this."

In his new book *Goodbye! Good Men*, Michael S. Rose documents in shocking detail how pervasive militant homosexuality is in many seminaries, how much gay sex is taking place among seminarians and priest-professors, and how gay power cliques exclude and punish heterosexuals who oppose them.

"It's not just a few guys in a few seminaries that have an ax to grind. It is a pattern," says Rose. "The protective network [of homosexual priests] begins in the seminaries."

The stories related in Rose's book will strike many as incredible, but they track closely with the stories that priests have told me about open gay sex and gay politicking in seminaries. The current scandal is opening Catholic eyes: As one ex-seminarian says, "People thought I was crazy when I told them what it was like there, so I finally quit talking about it. They're starting to see now that I wasn't [crazy]."

Further Complications

Goodbye! Good Men links homosexuality among priests with theological dissent, a connection commonly made by conservative Catholics who wonder why their parish priests have practically abandoned teaching and explaining Catholic sexual morality. But one veteran vocations team member for a conservative diocese cautions that Catholics should not assume that theological orthodoxy guarantees heterosexuality or chastity.

"You find [active homosexuality] among some pretty conservative orders, and in places you'd not expect it," he says. "That's what makes this so depressing. You don't know where to turn."

An especially nasty aspect of this phenomenon is the vulnerability of sexually active gay priests and bishops to manipulation via blackmail. Priests, psychiatrists, and other informed parties say they encounter this constantly. "It's the secrecy," says Stephen Rubino. "If you're a bishop and you're having a relationship, and people know about it, are you compromised on dealing with sexually abusive priests? You bet you are. I've seen it happen."

Longtime observers predict that in the coming weeks, bishops and priests will be forced to resign under fire after their closeted homosexual lives, including sexual abuse, become public. The disgraced pederast former bishop of Palm Beach, Florida, is probably not alone. If this happens, the Vatican will face mounting pressure from the Catholic rank-and-file to take action. As Fr. Greeley has written, "The laity, I suspect, would say it is one thing to accept a homosexual priest and quite another to accept a substantially homosexual clergy, many of whom are blatantly part of the gay subculture."

Should Homosexuals Be Ordained?

Rome has explicitly discouraged the ordination of homosexuals since at least 1961. For the past decade, the Vatican has been ratcheting up the pressure against gay ordination—to little avail in most U.S. dioceses.

Last year Archbishop Tarcisio Bertone, a top Vatican official, said gays should not be admitted to seminaries, a line that was reinforced in early March by the Pope's spokesman, Joaquin Navarro-Valls. Recent reports indicate that the Vatican may soon release another document to restate and clarify this policy.

Today, those who defend allowing homosexuals into the priesthood point to the Church's official teaching, which distinguishes between homosexual orientation (which the Church does not consider sinful) and homosexual acts (which the *Catechism* labels "grave depravity"). There is nothing wrong, the argument goes, with ordaining a homosexually oriented man committed to living chastely and to upholding the Church's teaching on sexuality. Surely there are many such faithful priests in service.

This argument, though, seems persuasive only under conditions far removed from those under which priests have to live today. We now have a culture in which there is little support for chastity, even from within the ranks of the Catholic priesthood. Conservative theologian Michael Novak says he is not prepared to argue for the exclusion of homosexuals from ordination, but as an ex-seminarian, he strongly believes gays should not be on seminary faculties, directing the formation in chastity of young men.

Other Catholics who are more liberal than Novak on many Church issues go further on the question of gay ordination: Sipe believes gays shouldn't be admitted into seminaries at the present time—for their own protection against sexual predators among the faculty and administration, who will attempt to draw them into a priestly subculture in which gay sex is normative behavior. Fr. Thomas P. Doyle, another critic of celibacy who has been deeply involved in the clergy abuse issue, concurs: "Ordaining gay men at this time would be putting them, no matter how good and dedicated, in a precarious position."

"We Have to Protect Our Young"

No one wants to stigmatize homosexuals as abusers, because most of them are not. Still, it's hard to gainsay the contention that if there were few homosexuals in the priesthood, the number of sex-abuse victims today would be drastically lower. "We're learning a significant lesson from all this," says Dr. Fitzgibbons. "We have to protect our young. The protection of children and teenagers is more important than the feelings of homosexuals."

Though the American scandal is nowhere near played out, it seems likely that the barrage of humiliating revelations and mounting financial losses will force the Vatican to get tough on gay ordinations. To have any hope of being effective, Rome will have to clean house at most American seminaries. This can be done only if local bishops can be trusted to be both loyal to Rome and resolute—and that will happen only if the Vatican forces them to be accountable.

That still leaves the problem of current and future priests who are both homosexual and unchaste. It is true that most of the abuse cases that have reached the public's attention today involve older priests, and the situation in the seminaries has apparently been reined in somewhat from the anything-goes heyday of the 1970s and 1980s. Nevertheless, the problem is still enormous.

Most of the cases reported in *Goodbye! Good Men* involving homosexual corruption date from recent years. One priest who left his seminary teaching post in the mid 1990s in despair over rampant homosexuality—and episcopal indifference to it—told me ominously: "The things I have seen in my years there are probably previews of coming attractions."

A Return to the Faith

The only sensible response, it would seem, is a zero-tolerance policy when it comes to sexual behavior by clergy, even between consenting adults (homosexual and heterosexual). The laity has a role to play as well. In a much-discussed essay in the November 2000 *Catholic World Report*, the Rev. Paul Shaughnessy, a Jesuit priest, suggested that lay Catholics seeking reform should help keep their priests accountable. He urged lay Catholics to use their checkbooks to fight sexual corruption, by steering their donations away from scandal-ridden dioceses and religious orders and sending them instead to clean groups like Mother Teresa's Missionaries of Charity—and then letting the bishop or religious order know what they've done and why.

There is tremendous fear among churchmen that the kind of changes needed to put the Church aright will result in a severe loss of numbers in the priesthood at a time when vocations are already at a historic low. That is probably true in the short run, but the experience of a handful of American dioceses in which the local bishop is openly orthodox and willing to defend Church teaching without compromise gives reason to hope that a strong dose of traditional medicine can go a long way toward curing the Church's ills.

In 1995, Archbishop Elden Curtiss of Omaha published an article pointing out that dioceses that promote rigorous fidelity to Church teaching and practice produce significantly more vocations than do the moderate to liberal majority. Seminaries like Mount Saint Mary's in Emmitsburg, Maryland—where men know they will be supported in their authentic Catholic beliefs and practices and in their commitment to celibacy and chastity—are filled to capacity.

This is not to suggest that the crisis now gripping the Catholic Church in America can be entirely solved by a restoration of rigorously orthodox theology. Another problem that has to be addressed is the clericalist bias seriously afflicting the judgment of many bishops: Even Curtiss himself erred recently, by keeping an Omaha priest in ministry after the priest admitted having a child-pornography problem.

But a return to the basics has to be a big part of a comprehensive solution. There is every reason to believe that a conservative reform—replacing dissenting or milquetoast bishops with solid, no-nonsense men; making the seminaries safe places for heterosexuals loyal to Church teaching; and restoring the priesthood to a corps of chaste, faith-filled disciples—would result in a tide of good men seeking holy orders.

This has already been happening in dioceses such as Omaha; Lincoln, Nebraska; Denver; Peoria, Illinois; Fargo, North Dakota; and Arlington, Virginia. The road map that points the way to an authentic renewal of the Catholic priesthood is being drawn up in those places. And if you want to see the alternative—what would happen if the U.S. Church simply stayed on its current course—just read the morning papers.

❖

Rod Dreher is a columnist for The National Review *(www.nationalreview.com). This essay is copyright 2002 by* The National Review *and first appeared in the April 22, 2002, issue of that publication. Used with permission.*

II: Responding to the Crisis

SEVEN

Sharing the Journey Toward Healing
How Can We Help the Victims?

Gregory K. Popcak

I know we were supposed to be talking about my marriage today, but I was wondering if you would mind if we changed the subject."

Marylin (not her real name), a client of mine through the Pastoral Solutions Institute, was in treatment for depression and marital problems, but it is not uncommon for clients to raise other topics during the course of treatment. I had no idea what was coming, but I told her that she was free to discuss whatever was on her heart. Having secured my permission for a change in our usual venue, she told me the following story.

"I have a cousin, Jerry, who is very bitter toward God and the Church. I always thought that was weird, because as a kid he always seemed to really 'get it' as far as religion went. Much more than I ever did.

"His folks fought a lot, and his dad cheated on his mom a lot. Eventually they split up, and his dad wasn't in the picture too much after that. Even though I'm sure that was hard on him, generally speaking, Jerry seemed pretty OK with it.

"He was always a good kid and never gave his mom any trouble. He was really active in their parish. He was an altar boy, he participated in the youth group, and he even thought about being a priest for a while.

"Then, when he got to high school, he just stopped caring about anything. He stopped going to Church, got into a bunch of trouble, ran away from home a lot. None of us ever wondered what was wrong. We just figured he fell in with the wrong crowd. It was the seventies and all.

"Anyway, he eventually settled down and got a regular job, though he never got married. Over the years, I've been trying to reach out to him and bring him back to the Church, maybe find him a nice girl or something, but he always turned me down when I asked him to come with me to different parish functions. He never told me why, and I never pushed.

"But this week I lost my patience with him. It had been a really tough week, and he called me in the middle of it just to talk. There was a Bible study just forming in our parish, and I thought he might be interested since it wasn't anything too Catholic. But he turned me down again, and I took it personally.

"I kept pushing him to tell me what his problem with the Church was, and we got into it. He finally started screaming at me. He told me that he didn't believe in God and that he never wanted to set foot in my [obscenity] Church ever again as long as he lived. And since I wanted to know why so badly, he would tell me.

"He said that Fr. Jack, our old pastor, couldn't keep his hands off him. That basically, he had molested Jerry over a dozen times in junior high and high school. When Jerry finally got strong enough to tell Fr. Jack off, Father told him that God had given him the power to forgive sins, but also to 'hold them bound,' and that if Jerry ever told anybody, he would hold Jerry's sins bound, and God would send him to hell.

"He told me that he tried to tell his mother, but he had a hard time, and when he finally got it out, she told him to stop telling stories. Fr. Jack had been a friend to the family after Jerry's father took off and had even lent his mother money and bought groceries over the years. She accused Jerry of talking crazy and told him that if he ever told lies like that again, she would throw him out. That was the first time he ran away from home."

Marylin didn't know what to do. She apologized profusely for having hounded Jerry all those years about coming to Church and begged him to forgive her. She told him how sorry she was, and he seemed to accept what she had to say, except that he hung up pretty quickly after that and hadn't called since, even though she'd left several messages. She felt terribly guilty and wondered how she should approach him, or even if she *should* approach him. She never imagined having to deal with anything like this, certainly not in her family, and certainly not involving a priest that she had known and liked.

Someone Near You May Be Hurting

The fact is, none of us are prepared for such an encounter. We can hear all the terrible things in the news about the abuse of young people by priests, but it is still a shock when we realize it has happened to someone we know and care about. But could it have really happened to someone you know?

Since so many of the incidents of priestly abuse occurred outside of the public eye, there are very few hard statistics that tell us how common this problem is. Just how many people have been affected?

The Linkup is a twelve-year-old organization whose mission is to support victims of priestly sexual abuse. *The Linkup* was founded by former Catholic priest Tom Economus, himself a victim of sexual abuse at the hands of a pastor. According to Economus, the number of victims could be staggering.

Using available statistics that estimate both the number of perpetrators among the U.S. priest population and the number of persons a sexual predator may victimize over the course of a lifetime, Economus suggests that the number of actual victims could be as high as one and a half million. Further, Economus adds that the number of people indirectly affected by the abuse of priests (for example, family members of victims who have had to deal with the emotional and relational costs of sexual abuse) could be as high as six million. If his estimates are correct, his total suggests that nearly 10 percent of the sixty-three million Catholics in the U.S. have been directly or indirectly affected by priestly sexual abuse.

Some take issue with Economus' figures, since he is not a social scientist and, in fact, has a high personal stake in the matter. For example, Economus assumed that at least 6 percent of priests are abusers, and that a single pedophile would victimize two hundred children in a lifetime. But sociologist Dr. Philip Jenkins' studies of the matter argue that the 6 percent figure is much too high. Based on his own detailed analysis of diocesan records, Jenkins states that only 2 percent of the population of priests are sexual predators.

But even if we did our own math with Jenkins' more conservative numbers, we see that there could be as many as nine hundred abusers among the active priests in the country (2 percent of the total priest population of forty-five thousand would be nine hundred). Likewise, considering what psychologists and sociologists know about the habits of sexual predators, it would not be unreasonable to assume that each one of these priests could have potentially abused as many as a hundred to a hundred and fifty children, for a grand total of as many as 100,000 to 150,000 children. Furthermore, assuming that there are about four to six people in the immediate family of the victim, we could safely suggest that as many as 400,000 to 900,000 people have been intimately, though indirectly, affected by priestly pedophilia in the United States alone, not counting friends and close associates of the victim.

In other words, there is a very good possibility that at some time in your life, you will encounter someone who has been abused by a priest. Would you know what to say or do?

How Can We Help?

I would offer the following suggestions for helping someone who has experienced abuse at the hands of a priest.

Listen

When we hear people speak of their suffering, we have a tendency to want to "help" them by offering pithy advice and comforting platitudes. "You're going to be OK." "Don't worry, time heals all wounds." "It happened a long time ago. You've got a good life now; just leave it in the past." "If there is anything I can do, let me know."

It pains us to see others' suffering, and we want to make it better. Unfortunately, none of these statements will make the victim of sexual abuse feel better. But there is still much you can do. You can listen.

Victims of sexual abuse experience profound shame and self-hatred. Deep inside, they often feel that they are dirty and unacceptable because of the frightening secrets they carry. This is truer still for the person who has been victimized by a priest. The victim of clergy abuse often says, "A man of God did this to me. What does that say about me in the eyes of God? If God allowed this to happen to me, how could others ever accept me?"

What people who have suffered abuse need most is another person who will listen to their story without panicking, becoming hysterical, or even wanting to take up a crusade on their behalf. They just want to have the experience of being able to speak the truth to someone who loves them, and still have that person love and accept them as a person. Not as a victim, not as a case, but as a friend.

Some helpful things you can say in the course of the conversation include the following:

"I want you to tell me whatever you are comfortable sharing with me."

"Thank you for sharing this with me. You can trust me with this."

"Will you let me be a part of whatever you need to do to heal?"

"What do you think you need to do to heal?"

Other questions along these lines can be supportive. Being an effective, active listener is key to helping victims of abuse know that they are loved and valuable in spite of whatever brokenness they may feel.

Be a Friend

Being a victim is a curious thing. Some days you want to shout from the rooftops, "I have been wounded. A terrible person did evil things to me! Help me!" Other days you just want others to see you as the normal, thinking, fun-loving, hopeful, kind, creative, and affectionate person you can be on your best days. Victims need to have their pain validated by others, but they also don't want to be identified solely by their pain.

Once you find out that your friend has been abused, let him know that this doesn't change a thing about your relationship. Don't let your friendship be swallowed up by her revelations. As time goes by, don't be afraid that he might not want to socialize; invite him to that party. Ask her if she wants to go to lunch.

Call, just to share a laugh. Let this person know that, in your eyes, he or she is still, first and foremost, a person. But try to be sensitive to your friend's moods. Is this a day he or she wants to discuss the pain, or is this a day that he or she just wants to be your friend?

If you don't know, simply say, "Listen, this is all really new to me. I want to give you whatever support you need, but I won't always know what you need and when. If I am reading you wrong, could you please promise to tell me whether today is a day that you need to talk about it, or if today is a day you'd rather just think about something else. I want to help, but I need you to take the lead in this. OK?"

Asking your friend to take the lead in the healing process is a very empowering thing. Chances are, he or she will chuckle about this being a case of the blind leading the blind. But your friend will appreciate both your honesty and your willingness to walk alongside, however blindly.

Know the Real Meaning of the Word *Forgive*

One of the biggest issues victims struggle with is the question of forgiveness. They know, and are told, that forgiveness is important to their spiritual walk, to their physical health, and to their to emotional healing. Unfortunately, victims are often repulsed at the idea of forgiving the "monster" who hurt them. At the same time, they may feel guilty for harboring their anger.

You can help by explaining to your friend what forgiveness really is. Forgiveness is nothing more than giving up your right to do harm to someone who has harmed you. That's it—a simple renunciation of your natural desire for revenge.

It doesn't mean the victim has to learn to be the abuser's best friend, and it doesn't mean that the victim has to let the abuser off the hook. St. Augustine once said that peace is "the tranquility that results from *right order*"(emphasis mine). In other words, if there is no justice, there is no peace.

Your friend has a natural right to see that right order is restored. Though your friend may forgive the abuser, the Church teaches that he or she still has a right to seek justice, in the form of proper punishment of the abuser, and the restoration of the sense of personal power and dignity. Again, all forgiveness means is that while seeing that true justice is served, your friend will not actively seek unjust or cruel punishment for the abuser.

Encourage Your Friend to Seek Professional Help

There is only so much you can do yourself. If you try to be your friend's sole support, you will be like someone who is not a strong swimmer trying to rescue a drowning man. In other words, there is a high likelihood that you could drown in your friend's pain as well.

No matter how good a support you are, your friend will absolutely need professional help at some point if he or she is not already receiving it. Because sexual abuse is such a painful wound to face, many victims will deny for years that they need help. I have had clients who have suffered in silence for ten, fifteen, twenty years or more before they sought help.

All that time they told themselves, "There's nothing I can do about it. I just have to get on with my life. I'm fine. Everything's fine." Often these people are highly efficient, super-performer types. In order to convince everyone and themselves that they are OK, they need to appear to be perfect. They often keep up this facade until they begin having uncontrollable panic attacks, unbearable depression, or rage, among other symptoms. Eventually, they can't keep it in anymore.

As you can see, at some point, your friend will need professional help to confront the pain successfully and resolve it. Offer to help your friend find someone. Offer to go to the first appointment and sit in the lobby if that would make the experience more comfortable. Additionally, many community mental health centers and women's shelters offer classes for helping friends and family members who have been sexually abused. Look into one of these classes for yourself, so that you can know how best to stand with your friend.

If your friend refuses your suggestions to seek professional help, don't push. Just keep your eyes open. If your friend is becoming consumed by anxiety, lost in depression, withdrawing from relationships and previously enjoyable activities, or constantly ruminating and obsessing over the abuse, this is a good sign that he or she has imminent need of professional assistance.

Gently mention your observations of such behavior, and respectfully suggest that it might be time to get help. In some cases it may take months, or even years, before your friend agrees with you. Be patient, be persistent, and be caring. In the long run, your efforts will pay off.

Pray

Only God can completely heal some wounds. The wound that results from sexual abuse at the hands of a priest is one such injury. Priestly sexual abuse is especially insidious because it robs people of three essential parts of their humanity: sexual innocence, personal power, and spiritual hope.

People who have suffered this kind of abuse, along with feeling "dirty," have a poor sense of personal power—for example, they may not know how to say no to inappropriate requests, they may be afraid to state opinions, or they may be extremely sensitive to the slightest criticism. In addition, they may harbor deep resentment toward God and hatred for the Church. Curiously, by contrast, some victims identify with their attackers and seek to become priests themselves. These individuals especially need professional help to sort out what is a legitimate spiritual call and what is merely the pathological playing out of a role written by a perpetrator.

The best way to bring your friend to a place of greater spiritual safety, health, and maturity is to model a healthy spirituality yourself. Confronting evil head-on has a way of making us turn more fully to God. Let your confrontation of the evil your friend has suffered draw you closer to the Lord.

Ask God to guide your steps, to give you his wisdom, and to help you lead your friend to God's love and healing. Ask God to send his healing Spirit to touch your friend's heart so that he or she can become the person God intends. Participate in the sacraments often, and be willing to share your experiences of God as healer, nurturer, protector, and friend. At the same time be sensitive to the fact that your friend may be wary of too much religious talk, since he or she does not personally experience God as healing, nurturing, protective, or friendly.

While you should feel free to invite your friend to attend church or other spiritual activities, often it is best to wait until he or she says something to you like, "How can you hold onto your faith knowing what you know about me?" Or even, "Why do you go to that church with all those hypocrites and perverts?" Respond to these challenges as honestly and gently as you can, but make sure that you listen mostly.

Feel free gently to challenge such in-your-face comments with charitable questions like "Do you think that I am a hypocrite?" You might say, "I can hold on to my faith because I know what the Church really is and what it is not. The priest who did this to you was merely pretending. He was using the props of religion to meet his own evil ends, but religion itself is a good gift, given by a God who loves us." As with suggesting professional help, proceed cautiously, gently, and persistently when trying to lead your friend back to the Lord or the Church.

Relax, and Be Willing to Make It Up as You Go

While there is much more that will need to be said and done in the course of your relationship with your friend, these suggestions can start you out on the right path. Traveling down this path will require sensitivity and a willingness to listen to the unique needs of your friend, since no two people heal in exactly the same way. Avoid cookie-cutter approaches to healing, and be wary of any "expert" who tells you that such approaches exist.

In short, the better a listener, friend, cheerleader, supporter, and intercessor you can be, the more God can work through you to bring your friend into the fullness of his healing love.

The most important tip that I can leave you with, however, is just to remember to relax. God put you in your friend's life at this time because God felt that you were just the right person for the job, simply because you are who you are. Trust that God knows what he is doing, and be the best friend you can be to this man or woman who, right at this moment, needs a faithful—and faith-filled—friend more than anything else.

✦

Gregory K. Popcak, MSW, LISW, is the director of the Pastoral Solutions Institute and author of five books on psychology and the Catholic faith. He has personally conducted thousands of hours of telephone counseling with Catholics around the world. For more information, go online to www.exceptionalmarriages.com.

EIGHT

Operation Plainspeak
An Open Letter to the American Bishops

The Editors of *Catholic World Report*

Your Excellencies,

At your June meeting you will discuss the scandal that has enveloped the Catholic Church in the United States. As faithful Catholics we feel an obligation to raise our voices, to raise this respectful plea for plain speech and bold leadership.

The severity of this crisis should not be underestimated. This scandal has not been created by the mass media; secular reporters have merely exposed the unhappy truth, uncovering a frightening pattern of abuse and corruption within the Church.

The results have been catastrophic. The Church has been exposed to public ridicule. The laity have become increasingly angry, confused, and demoralized. Worst of all, the work of evangelization has been hindered, and salvation of souls has been jeopardized.

In recent weeks some aspects of this scandal have been discussed exhaustively: the psychological suffering endured by the victims of priestly sexual abuse; the financial consequences of lawsuits against various dioceses; the prospects for criminal prosecution of some clerics. All of these factors deserve serious attention.

But as successors to the Apostles, you must make the spiritual welfare of the community your paramount concern. How many young people have been led into sinful acts by Catholic priests? How many other clerics have ignored the clear evidence of wrongdoing and thus given their tacit consent to gravely immoral acts? How many people have been turned away from the Catholic faith by this scandal?

A public scandal calls for a public response. You, as leaders of the Catholic Church in America, must speak and act decisively to repair the grave damage that our Church has suffered.

Recognizing the Problem

The problems that we face have been caused, in no small part, by a failure to act forthrightly: to acknowledge inconvenient facts and to deal with unwelcome truths. As you address these problems today you must face the facts squarely and proclaim the truth boldly—confident in the knowledge that "the truth will set you free" (see Jn 8:32).

Media accounts regularly identify the current scandal as a matter of "priestly pedophilia." But that description is not accurate, for two reasons.

First, the sexual misbehavior of Catholic priests is only one part of the current crisis. The problem has been compounded, and the scandal has been exacerbated, by the failure of Church leaders to intervene to stop the sexual abuse. The flagrant and widespread abdication of pastoral responsibility has shown a deep corruption with the American hierarchy. In many ways the tepid response to priestly sexual abuse has been more scandalous than the abuse itself.

Second, the sexual misconduct of American priests has not been confined to pedophilia—that is, the abuse of young children. In the vast majority of cases, the priests' victims have been adolescent boys or young men. Emerging evidence makes it impossible to ignore the widespread toleration of homosexual activity among American priests.

This widespread acceptance of homosexual activity is a grave problem in itself because it causes disdain for Catholic doctrine and fosters a climate of hypocrisy among those who are the official representatives of Church teaching.

We believe that the current scandal is a direct consequence of a failure to uphold and promote the teachings of the Catholic Church regarding sexual morality. When bishops do not accept, understand, and boldly proclaim the necessary link between sexual intimacy and procreation, they cannot expect the faithful of their dioceses to uphold that magisterial teaching.

Once that crucial link between sexual intimacy and procreation has been severed, there is no compelling justification for the restriction of intimacy to marriage or to partners of the opposite sex. There may be some remaining cultural barriers to sexual activity outside of marriage, but those barriers crumble all too quickly in the face of temptation— especially for individuals who have not accepted the teachings of the Church and made a determined effort to develop the virtue of chastity.

At a time when our society has been battered by the "sexual revolution" and its aftermath, very few Catholic leaders have been clear and consistent in their proclamation of the truth about human sexuality. Rather than risking public controversy, many bishops and priests have chosen a "pastoral approach," avoiding any public mention of Church teachings that have become unfashionable. The disastrous results of that "pastoral approach" have been evident for years in the breakdown of American family life. Now it is even more painfully apparent in the scandal of priestly sexual misconduct.

Accepting Responsibility

The problem that you must now confront cannot be solved simply by adopting new procedures and guidelines for the handling of troubled priests. Still less can it be solved by setting "boundaries" for clerical behavior, as some commentators have suggested. Guidelines and procedures are useless if they are not enforced; "boundaries" will soon be crossed by clerics who lack the habits of chastity and self-discipline.

The resolution of this crisis will begin, we respectfully suggest, when you, our bishops, firmly insist that the teachings of the Church must be upheld ... and the discipline of the Church must be enforced, in the seminaries, parishes, and schools under your authority.

Many Church leaders, in their failure to respond to clerical misconduct, have abdicated their solemn responsibility to the faithful. (We make this charge with regret, but recent public revelations have made the situation painfully clear, and we shall not shrink from the facts.) In some cases, bishops and other diocesan officials have become complicit partners in sexual abuse.

Those individuals—regardless of their rank—should resign from their positions, in recognition of their culpability. If they do not voluntarily resign, they must be removed.

Many American bishops have issued public apologies to the faithful for the scandal of sexual abuse. Such apologies are necessary but not sufficient. Accepting responsibility means not only assuming blame for a problem but also assuming the moral burden of solving that problem. Again, this scandal calls for decisive moral leadership.

A Plan of Action

An effective plan to end this scandal, and to root out the corruption within the Church in America, must include three essential elements:

1. *No one should assume any position of authority in the Church (including admission to Holy Orders or religious vows, appointment as religious superior or director of formation, or employment in any decision-making position within a diocesan chancery) who does not accept and publicly defend all the teachings of the Catholic Church.*

A vague or general statement of fealty to the Catholic faith is not an adequate indication of doctrinal reliability. Anyone worthy of leadership in the Church must offer public assent to the more controversial elements of Catholic doctrine—for instance, the following propositions from the *Catechism of the Catholic Church:*

"Only a baptized man (*vir*) validly receives sacred ordination" (*Codex Iuris Canonici,* 1024).... For this reason the ordination of women is not possible.

CCC 1577

Basing itself on Sacred Scripture, which presents homosexual acts as acts of grave depravity,[1] tradition has always declared that "homosexual acts are intrinsically disordered" (Congregation for the Doctrine of the Faith, *Persona humana,* 8).... Under no circumstances can they be approved.

CCC 2357

> The Church ... teaches that "it is necessary that each and every marriage act remain ordered *per se* to the procreation of human life" (*Humanae Vitae* 11).
>
> *CCC* 2366

2.Everyone who undertakes a position of authority in the Church must resolve to enforce the teaching and discipline of the Church and demand the same resolve from those who are under his authority.

Moral leadership begins, rather than ends, with the statement of principles. A conscientious leader must assure himself, to the best of his ability, that his subordinates put those principles into action.

The father of a human family is rightly judged irresponsible if he ignores—and thus appears to condone—serious crimes committed by his children. By the same token, a bishop, pastor, or religious superior must be judged seriously negligent if he does not respond to gravely sinful actions committed under the scope of his authority. A shepherd must use his powers, when necessary, to keep the wayward members of his flock from straying and to repel the predators who threaten them.

The willingness to tackle difficult problems, and impose necessary discipline, should be recognized as a sign of the capacity for leadership. Priests who have demonstrated their willingness to endure controversy should be rewarded with greater responsibilities; those who have shrunk from the proper exercise of their own legitimate authority should not be considered for higher offices.

Effective pastoral leadership entails not only addressing moral problems but also encouraging the practice of virtues. Church leaders should provide steady, concrete, and practical guidance for those under their authority. Thus, for example, bishops should encourage their priests to maintain a properly ordered and disciplined life, which should include:

- the regular use of the sacraments, especially frequent confession
- a rigorous program of prayer and spiritual direction
- moderation in the use of alcohol and prudence in the choice of forms of recreation
- the maintenance of a regular, disciplined daily work schedule
- the diligent avoidance of occasions of sin
- careful cultivation of a dignified public manner, avoiding even the appearance of impropriety

3. *Church leaders must make a firm commitment to be diligent in investigating any credible evidence of dissent from defined doctrine or violation of moral norms, within the scope of their authority.*

Whenever a Church leader receives evidence that serious offenses have been committed under his jurisdiction—whether it is homosexual activity at a seminary, alcoholic behavior in a rectory, or heterodox teaching at a Catholic college—he has a heavy obligation to investigate the charges promptly and thoroughly.

Anonymous accusations should not be encouraged. But if an individual member of the faithful comes forward with substantive evidence of wrongdoing, he deserves a respectful hearing.

Regrettably, many faithful Catholics in America today have reached the conclusion that their bishops will not address their complaints until they are forced to do so by adverse publicity. In some cases, bishops and other Church leaders owe apologies to those faithful Catholics who have carefully assembled the evidence of clerical wrongdoing, doing their best to avoid public scandal—only to have their efforts dismissed, and their own integrity questioned, by the officials to whom they addressed their legitimate concerns.

Lay people have the legitimate right to know that their pastors take their concerns seriously. Parents have the right to demand that their children are receiving proper moral formation and adequate protection. Pastors should always recognize that parents are the primary educators of their own children—particularly regarding matters involving sexuality.

Circumstantial evidence of misbehavior should not ordinarily be grounds for disciplinary action; on the other hand, such evidence should not be ignored. A priest whose behavior gives rise to concerns among his parishioners should be required to provide a thorough and convincing explanation for that behavior.

If the evidence of wrongdoing is compelling, the offender must be punished. In order to make a clear moral statement, and avoid the appearance of hypocrisy, Church leaders should make no effort to conceal the true reasons for removal of an official who has been implicated in a public scandal.

Be Assured of Our Prayers

We recognize that this program will place new demands on the Catholic faithful, lay and religious, as well as on bishops and priests. We stand ready and willing to undertake the commitments, and make the sacrifices, that we enjoin upon you.

During your June meeting, as you plan your response to this crisis, be assured of our prayerful support for your efforts and our willingness to follow your decisive leadership in a bold program of spiritual restoration and moral reform.

✦

This letter originally appeared in the May 2002 issue of Catholic World Report *(www.cwnews.com/cwreport), copyright 2002 by Domus Enterprises. Used with permission.*

---

1. Cf. Gen 19:1-29; Rom 1:24-27; 1 Cor 6:10; 1 Tim 1:10.

NINE

Dark Hour
The Long Good Friday of 2002

Mark Shea

On Good Friday 2002, it was as bad as it looked—and as of this writing it still is. Fr. John Geoghan has been convicted of child rape and molestation. Over ninety civil lawsuits against Geoghan and the archdiocese of Boston, stemming from Geoghan's three decades of alleged rape and abuse of over 130 Boston-area children, have yet to come to trial. That, of course, is bad enough. But it gets worse.

As we all now know, the Boston hierarchy had asked the families of victims to keep it quiet, promised that everything would be taken care of—and then reassigned and reshuffled and reassigned Geoghan (and allegedly many others like him) to parishes where he was in direct contact with children and where he continued to commit his crimes for nearly two decades. Worse still, the ex-bishop of Palm Beach, Anthony O'Connell (who was himself brought into the Palm Beach diocese to replace a bishop who was a sexual molester), resigned when it came to light that he had molested a boy who had already been molested by two other priests.

Now there are serious questions about the handling of cases by Cardinal Edward Egan of New York, Cardinal Roger Mahony of Los

Angeles, and various others. And perhaps most egregious of all (though it's so hard to choose infamies in such a target-rich environment), we learned that a creature like "Fr." Paul Shanley, advocate for the North American Man-Boy Love Association, could continue his evil career for twenty years, raping boys and publicly advocating sex with minors, as his cowardly bishops not only looked the other way but even gave him glowing recommendations while hiding his seamy activities from unsuspecting people.

This constitutes the gravest breakdown in moral credibility the American Catholic hierarchy has ever faced. For many, the year 2002 has felt like Good Friday in a way we've never known before. It was and is a black hour.

Make no mistake. There is, quite simply, no excuse for this. And nobody—not even the pit-bull-like defenders of the faith at the Catholic League or stalwart Catholics such as William F. Buckley or William Bennett—is making any. Faithful Catholics are simply appalled by the gravity of the sins of such priests and of the sins of bishops whose first thought appears to have been informed by (a) world-class folly or (b) the rankest clericalism, which insisted on protecting members of the priestly guild from problems but not protecting innocent children from sexual predators.

The tremors from this and other cases like it continue sending shock waves through the American Church. Some have written me to say, "My family and I have left the Church and have no intention of providing financial support for any Catholic organization until the Church cleans up its act!" Others have written to say, in effect, "It's all a media plot to discredit the Church! Where were they when Clinton was pulling his hijinks?" Still others have written to say simply, "What do we do?"

Thinking Informed With Revelation

My answer is this: I empathize completely with people in their disgust over the behavior of both the priests and the bishops who have so egregiously sinned in creating this inexcusable scandal. The priests who engaged in scandalous behavior should be removed from their offices and, where crimes have been committed, punished according to the law. Bishops who repeatedly and knowingly lied to victims and exposed still more victims to the depredations of these men should face the consequences of their actions.

In such an hour, it is vital for Catholics to inform their thinking with revelation, not just newspapers and TV, and not just political inclination, whether left- or right-wing. One extremely common blunder which causes endless confusion is failure to distinguish between the hierarchy and the Church. When John Paul II, in his "Letter to Priests" for Holy Thursday 2002, said, "The Church shows her concern for the victims and strives to respond in truth and justice to each of these painful situations," many people cried, "But the Church has been abusing people, not responding in truth!"

This shows clearly one vital thing that many Catholics have failed to grasp: Neither Scripture nor Tradition permits us to reduce "the Church" to "the hierarchy," nor "the hierarchy" to a merely political entity. The Church is the mystical body of Christ. The hierarchy is integral to that Body as a skeleton is. But just as you are more than your skeleton, so the Body of Christ is more than the hierarchy.

The Church (that is, the body of Christ) is indeed the victim of this abuse and does indeed strive to respond in truth and justice. For the soul of the Church is the Holy Spirit, not the hierarchy. In each child that is abused, Jesus Christ—and therefore his body which is the

Church—is abused. That is why Jesus tells us, "Inasmuch as you did it to the least of these, you did it to me" (see Mt 25:40), and said to Paul, who was persecuting nameless faceless Christians, "Saul, Saul, why do you persecute me?" (see Acts 9:4).

Very well, then, members of the Church in the ordained office have committed abuse. But the Church—that is, the mystical body of Christ—did not commit abuse. It bears the wounds of Christ, and he, with wounded hands, reaches out in compassion to those who have been harmed.

Another point (just to clear the air of the normal "Ha! The Church doesn't look so infallible now, does it?" rhetoric): The bishop's three-fold task is to teach, govern, and sanctify. Note that the failure of the hierarchy in this instance is a failure of governance, not doctrine (which is all infallibility protects).

The blunder of the hierarchy is not that they promote an "antiquated" doctrine of sexual chastity that needs to change to fit the current notions of the editorial board of the *New York Times,* as the theologically challenged columnists Maureen Dowd and Anna Quindlen foolishly inform us. Rather, it means that some in the hierarchy have permitted a culture of contempt for chastity and orthodoxy to grow up in the educational and bureaucratic machinery of the American Church (indeed, some have even participated in that culture) with utterly predictable results.

This constitutes the difference between the anger that orthodox Catholics feel over this scandal and the endless carping of the dissenters. Dissenters demand that the Church abandon its doctrine. Faithful Catholics demand that the Church—including its bishops and priests—*live* its doctrine.

How Should We Respond?

Keeping in mind, then, that we must pay attention to revelation, not politics and polls, in weighing this matter, faithful Catholics can and do disagree on just what the consequences should be for bishops who have badly mishandled their office in this case.

Now, the Church is not (despite the conviction of Americans to the contrary) a democracy. And this is so not because sinister Italian prelates opposed to truth, justice, and the American way are strangling the noble yearnings for freedom that beat in the breast of every oppressed lay Catholic on earth. It's so because Jesus of Nazareth set up a hierarchical Church.

As a layman, I can and do have opinions about what should be done. But I do not possess authority from Christ to force my opinions on the Church. I accept this with docility and advocate no anticlerical movement. But I also believe that my Lord wishes me to think with the Tradition and to speak the truth in love. So here goes:

First, I empathize strongly with the fact that the Good Shepherd lays down his life for the sheep. Each day a bishop who was spectacularly negligent, or who stonewalled, or who played brutal legal hardball with victims rather than take seriously the very credible charges of rape, abuse, and molestation—each day such a bishop clings to office is a day in which the scandal grows and the moral credibility of the American Catholic hierarchy dwindles into invisibility. And so, from a purely off-the-cuff practical perspective, my first thought is that such bishops should go.

There are arguments against this, some of them bad ones in my opinion. The worst of these goes: "Even thinking such a thing puts us on a 'slippery slope' toward mob rule of the Church. If today a bishop resigns for this scandal, then tomorrow it will be fifty other bishops over far less serious offenses or imagined offenses, if only a mob can be whipped up."

I disagree. Catholics have been extraordinarily slow to want to believe the worst of their shepherds. Indeed, it has taken offenses of this gravity to get Catholics passionate enough to speak. What we want—no, what we *need*, dear fathers in the faith, anointed by God Most High—is trusty shepherds, not the French Revolution. And so some ask, not with the violent and power-seeking ultimatums of man but with the humility of Christ, that if you cannot be that for us, if you cannot do your office, then for the sake of him who emptied himself for our salvation, let the one who can do that office fill your shoes. I can empathize with this opinion strongly and am not at all convinced that it will not prevail—nor that it shouldn't.

What Is the Pope Thinking?

Nevertheless, the Pope does not seem to share my opinion and has not only *not* asked for any resignations from our bishops but has refused them (except in the case of the clearly criminal O'Connell and the already retiring Weakland). This gives me real pause. Indeed, since John Paul is neither a fool nor a wicked man but a man profoundly steeped in the Tradition, this troubled me deeply—till I had a conversation recently with a very thoughtful and profound friend that has made me think twice about my "throw 'em out" instant reaction to The Situation.

This friend is a priest, the soul of common sense, and probably the closest I will ever get to meeting St. Thomas Aquinas. He is habitually cool and sane in his judgments and also deeply informed by the Tradition. In the course of our conversations, I have become deeply convinced that he is right in his assessment of the Pope's thinking. And I think it will have to inform the way we lay people approach this crisis too, if the Church is to ever to find our way back out of the woods.

Padre observes that the problem here is not "failure to consult the laity." Laity, he noted, *have* been consulted all through the past two decades. The problem is this: The laity consulted were lawyers and psychologists.

Tremendous attention was paid to various secular models of doing business, evaluating problem priests, dealing with threats of lawsuit, and so on. What nobody has paid attention to is the *Tradition* and what revelation says about the nature of the office of priest.

Cardinal Mahony's breathtakingly shallow response is to hire a PR firm to fix his skin-deep "image," rather than to address the soul-deep problem of his wretched treatment of victims and reassignment of abusers. Cardinal Egan acts like a bureaucrat of the Reich, smashing victims in court and using Clintonian legal tactics to try to claim that the priests for which he is responsible before God are "independent contractors." Heck, in Seattle, where I live, the bishop's letter to the archdiocese about The Situation closed with a reference, not to Scripture, but to Elisabeth Kubler-Ross.

The bishops have forgotten the Tradition they should be teaching and are flailing about in secular models and paradigms, trying to get a clue about what they are supposed to be doing.

"I begin," Padre says, "with the rather obvious evidence that Cardinal Law is not a bad man. So how did he get to where he is?" His diagnosis, in a nutshell, is that the vast majority of American bishops simply have no clue what the office of priest means and have forgotten that they are priests, thinking rather that they are the CEOs of corporations and running their dioceses on models derived, not from a revealed understanding of their offices found in the Tradition, but from purely secular templates.

Thus, when something arises that threatens the smooth running of the machine, the bishops think first of guarding the machinery of institution while forgetting what the institution exists to do. After all, "qualified experts" have counseled them to do exactly this, and they want to be "responsive." Yes, that *is* what's going through their heads.

Christ Himself Is Wounded

What has not been named in this scandal, he said, is that the first one wounded in this is Jesus Christ, not the institution and not even the victims. It is the sacrament of Holy Orders that has been blasphemed, and *this is greater even than the crimes against children and other innocents.* For Jesus Christ is peculiarly present in the sacrament of the priest and in the priest's victims. In committing these crimes, the gravest sin involved in this blasphemy is therefore not abuse of children, horrible as that is. It is that such sin denies people access to Christ, grotesquely deforms our ability to see him, or blinds us to him altogether.

This diagnosis, though counterintuitive, is simply right, I think. Children are not the primary victims of these sins: Jesus Christ is. And he is so precisely because he is present both in the children and families wounded and in the sacrament of Holy Orders, which criminal priests and their protective bishops share.

This disconnect between the AmChurch bishops' conception of

their office and the Holy Father's is, said my priest friend, quite clear and obvious to the Holy Father. My friend has been rereading the *ad limina* addresses John Paul gave to our bishops in the late nineties, and as you might expect, the Pope has a markedly different conception—what some of us might call a *Catholic* conception—of the ordained office as being a shepherd of souls, not a CEO of a large corporation.

But now the need for a more Traditional (mark that: "Traditional," not "reactionary" or "conservative," since these are also secular political categories that are not rooted in the Tradition) conception of the nature of Holy Orders as ordaining shepherds and not CEOs is suddenly making itself felt in exquisite ways to our bishops. And ironically, I find that my initial conception of what to do about things ("Replace defective Part A with functional Part B to fix administrative machinery") is remarkably closer to Bill Gates' than to the Holy Father's or my priest friend's.

"The first blunder," said Padre, "was to yank abusive priests out before they had the chance to face the people they'd hurt." He did not mean they should be left in place to harm more kids. Those priests (like Shanley or Geoghan) who did the crime should do the time.

But in addition to handing them over to civil authorities, said my friend, it should be Church policy to allow their parishes and victims to confront abusers in some sort of parish meeting so that abusers can receive the full wrath (and the possibility of mercy and reconciliation) from the people they've hurt. Simply yanking them in the dead of night truncated the possibility of a victim's working through his or her anger to forgiveness and positively encouraged abusers to think they were immune to the consequences of their actions. *To be a priest is to carry the cross, not to take a powder. And that includes crosses they themselves made and laid on the shoulders of their victims.*

And this explains very well, I think, why John Paul leaves the present crop of bishops in their jobs to endure and carry the cross they have created and laid on the shoulders of so many innocent people. My priest friend thinks that the Holy Father believes that this is the time when abusive American clergy are going to have to carry the cross they made for others so that the American Church (both laity and clergy) learn what the true nature of priesthood is supposed to be. Simply thinking in secular categories and treating this as an administrative machinery problem will not serve.

The problem here is the failure to grasp the nature of the sacrament, and yanking these bishops off the crosses they now occupy will only be another manifestation of such thinking. It will mean that abusers and the bishops who sheltered them don't really face the consequences of their actions and that they will be replaced by more people who have no more conception of the nature of their priestly office than their predecessors did.

I find this argument very compelling. So in the end I am forced to conclude that, despite the gravity of the crisis now engulfing the American Catholic Church, demands for the resignation of bishops who have so terribly and sinfully mismanaged the Church and permitted such terrible wounding of their flocks are not, in fact, the wisest approach (except, of course, in the case of actual criminal activity by the bishop).

Avoiding Two Extremes

I think this with fear and trembling and with full awareness that, if this is the case, the Holy Father is taking a risk, not issuing a dogma. I'm not unaware of the danger of revolutionary extremism seething out there. There are indeed two extremes to which we can slide in our response to such sins as have been committed by the members of our Church who share in the sacrament of Holy Orders. We can abandon Christ in his darkest hour, or we can make excuses for Judas Iscariot and blame everybody but him for his sins. Both extremes betray the body of Christ.

The Church, the whole company of the faithful in union with the bishops and Peter, is the body of Christ. But as St. Teresa of Avila says, Christ has no hands on earth now but ours. If we simply bail on the Church, we are effectively cutting off some of Christ's fingers while expecting him to do more work. Better to remain with the Church and labor against sins than just to pull out and make the job all that harder for Catholics who are trying to clean things up.

On the other hand, if we "fight for the Church" by trying to deny that it's as bad as it looks, and make excuses for these priests and the bishops who have coddled them, we simply perpetuate the problem. So it seems to me we lay people are bound to speak out and to act— and likewise to carry the cross. But we are bound to do so in such a way as neither to enable the problem nor to injure the body of Christ.

If it has been clearly shown that your diocese is involved in these shenanigans, then I know of nothing in the *Catechism of the Catholic Church* that forbids you from tithing to your local parish but sending your diocesan contributions somewhere else, to somebody who is doing good works rather than committing or enabling criminal acts. I don't see why a layperson can't write a letter to his bishop explaining his actions or expressing what's on his heart. If the Apostles could speak their heart and mind with Christ, surely we lay folk can do so with our pastors. But whatever we do, we can't just stop being generous. We must be generous where it will do good, donating to worthy apostolates.

Likewise, though we should obviously be praying for the victims of this abuse and helping them as we can, we must also never stop praying for the clergy who sinned against them. Never withhold forgiveness from them. Unforgiveness is the short road to spiritual suicide. For this sin, like all sin, though of course it cannot be excused, can and must be forgiven.

Further, if you are teaching or bearing witness to the faith, don't feel as though "defending the faith" is identical with "making excuses for the behavior of sexual predators and the bishops who shelter them." So, for example, although it is true that other denominations and demographic groups have similar rates of abuse, don't use this as a way to excuse the Catholic leaders for their inexcusable behavior in failing to protect their flocks.

At the same time, be suspicious of media hysteria and agitation propaganda. Defending the faith means (at the very least) abiding by the simple canons of civil justice, which hold among other things that the accused is innocent until proven guilty. Not every accusation is true merely because it is alleged. There will be those who will make false charges just for the money.

In addition, there are thousands who are interested in using this scandal to advance agendas having little or nothing to do with it. There are also those who don't wish to connect some rather uncomfortable dots: for example, that 90 percent of the cases of abuse are homosexual in nature, and that this indicates strongly that the Standard Media Template of the gay subculture as a happy, healthy "alternative lifestyle" consists of a huge amount of smoke and mirrors. Every time someone regurgitates what some Talking Hairdo on TV tells him and cries out, "Celibacy causes these perversions! If priests were allowed to marry, they wouldn't do these sick things!" ask if he really *means* to say homosexuals aren't genetically determined and can change. The shattering sound you'll hear is two Standard Media Templates smashing into each other at high velocity.

None of this, I repeat, is to excuse the inexcusable. Members of the ordained office have done evil and must be called to account for it and bear the consequences of their actions. The time is long past for them to bear the cross they have so long neglected in order finally to begin doing their office. The time is long past for them to do something about the culture of contempt for chastity and sound Catholic teaching in the bureaucratic and educational structures of the Church. The time is long past for them to understand what it means to be a priest, to do their office, and to bear the sufferings they have so callously inflicted on others so that the damage they have done might be healed.

At the same time, we lay people must do our office, too, not simply cut ourselves off from the whole Church in a blind fury or pretend it's all no big deal. The former course helps nothing and simply impoverishes us and our families of any contact with the sacraments (and wrongly blames the entire Church *en masse* for the sins of a few). The latter endangers still more innocent people by telling abusers and their protectors that there is no consequence for their actions.

God's Covenant Remains

In the Old Testament the God-anointed King of Israel, David, committed adultery with Bathsheba and then murdered her husband, Uriah. It was, like the Boston case and others, as bad as it looked.

David had no excuses. And he was punished for his sins—as was proper (see 2 Sm 11:1–12:25).

This punishment meant many things, but the one thing it did not mean was that the people of Israel were no longer chosen by God. God's covenant is not dependent on how good or bad we are; it's dependent on his faithfulness. Same here. The fact that some bishops and priests (some—by no means all or even most) have committed egregious and inexcusable sin does not mean that the Church is not the Church, or that God's covenant is not still in effect.

To abandon that covenant is, in reality, simply to allow evil in the Church to take another victim: you. Don't let it. Stay and fight for the culture of life to prevail in the Church. That's not rebellion; that's obedience.

The Church has been through other, far darker Good Fridays. God brought Easter then. He will do it again.

Mark Shea is senior content editor at CatholicExchange.com, a nonprofit web portal for Catholics. An award-winning columnist and best-selling author, his most recent book is Making Senses Out of Scripture: Reading the Bible as the First Christians Did *(Basilica).*

TEN

A Chill in the Church's Springtime
The Challenges Posed for Faithful Priests

Fr. Mitchell C. Pacwa, S. J.

These days, faithful priests have to deal with considerable fallout from the sexual abuse committed by other priests and bishops. The lack of a satisfactory response from the hierarchy adds to the pain and confusion.

Of course, accounts of sexual abuse by priests of a few children and many adolescents have been appearing in the American media from time to time since 1985. At first, the great majority of priests and bishops were blindsided by the initial shock that a priest would so harm a child. Now the early years of the new millennium have brought a jolting chill into the Church's springtime, as the press dedicates large amounts of air time and print to the issue, exposing numerous criminal cases, even on a daily basis.

Difficulties Faced

Faithful priests face a number of difficulties in this difficult situation. First, they feel a horrible sense of dismay at such behavior by their own. When I was a boy, my heroes—Hopalong Cassidy, Gene Autry, and Roy Rogers—gave way in time (mostly, not entirely) to the young associate priests I knew, and even to the usually much-feared pastor. For most of us, priest heroes awakened our vocations at an early age and sustained our vocations during the long course of discernment and studies for the priesthood. We wanted to be like these good men who served God and neighbor unselfishly, men who were respected for their generosity, intelligence, and religious leadership.

The fact that brother priests—whom I still want to admire—would hurt the children I love and want to serve is thus an excruciating pain. No wonder so many of us feel embarrassment these days at appearing in public dressed in clerical clothes.

The great majority of our parishioners continue to respond to us with love for the priesthood and for those of us who serve our parishes. The people continue to attend Mass, greet us warmly, and frequently say, "Thank you for being a priest." I cannot be grateful enough for their support.

While walking through malls or airports, however, the eyes of some people follow me, not with respect for the priesthood but with a look of suspicion. As I was boarding a plane recently, a woman standing near me, thinking it a joke, asked me, "Abused any kids today, Father?" I had not expected that, and I had no answer. She suddenly realized that her quip was not really funny, and she apologized as I continued down the walkway to the plane.

A priest friend of mine was shopping when another person said, "Shame, shame, shame!" as he waited at the checkout counter. He thought faster than I would have, and he asked to see her hand. Then he pointed out that even though all five appendages on her hand were fingers, not all were the same size. She immediately grasped the analogy and apologized.

A far more painful reality is the criticism of priests endured by the laity at school and work. Adolescents are not especially adept at making distinctions based on careful observation of facts. Children, especially boys, are often harassed by peers who consider all priests pedophiles. No priest wants his parishioners to experience such embarrassment over the sins of other members of the Church, so this becomes another source of pain over which there is little control.

Yet another problem is that many of us priests now feel self-conscious when we are with children. The vast majority of us, of course, have no desire to abuse young people. But suspicion of our desire to teach or show affection toward children has become a pollution in the ministerial environment.

Financial Challenges

Finally, priests often feel embarrassment about the large sums of money that have been paid to the victims of child abuse. After all, this money was not earmarked for priests in the first place but for the ministry to which we have given our lives. Its misuse is a terrible injustice.

While some voices in the media speak about the need to cause the Church great financial pain in order to force the hierarchy to take responsibility for the crimes committed, we priests who work within the Church have another perspective. We see that such measures would be taken at the expense of schools and individual churches. Present buildings dedicated to worship of God and service to our neighbor might have to be sold to pay the huge settlements being demanded.

Ironically, the perpetrators are not the ones paying out this money.

Nor is it drawn from the private funds of the bishops. It is money that was given by the people of God for other, more admirable purposes: to serve the poor and needy, to educate our children in the faith, and to build beautiful churches.

Perhaps we priests have become too comfortable, but I think most of us would willingly sacrifice whatever comforts we have in order to help the Church out in this crisis. Nonetheless, even if we priests pooled our resources, we could not begin to pay the punitive damages in the lawsuits of our offending brothers. Nor can we afford on our own to build new churches, schools, and hospitals, no matter how much we might sacrifice personal comforts. So we must continue to ask for more money to support our apostolates. But we feel embarrassed to do so because we cannot always explain the allocation of the money donated.

All these challenges—the dismay, the embarrassment, the public suspicion, the financial uncertainties—seem of course like small burdens compared to the agony suffered by those who have been directly victimized by the abusers. Many of us have simply concluded that we need to accept these trials as splinters of the cross we bear as priests. And since the problems we face are the result of real abuse by those with whom we have identified, we must see this cross not so much as persecution for the sake of the holiness of the faith but as a pain due to the sin of other Christians, particularly our brother priests.

Dealing With Offending Priests

At certain moments we priests certainly feel tremendously angry with the perpetrators of sexual abuse of children, but mostly we have concern for them. We may have been trained with them or by them; they may have been longtime friends with whom we took vacations; they may have been coworkers in a parish; they may even have heard our confessions or given us spiritual direction.

Furthermore, we know that we ourselves are sinners in various ways. Perhaps this particular sin seems more serious than ours, but we still want to have compassion on the abusers.

No doubt, on the one hand, our first duty—and the duty of the hierarchy—is to protect children from any further sexual abuse. Much more important than our embarrassment, anger, or disappointment is the safety of the children. We must do everything possible to prevent further crimes.

The victims have suffered a grave objective evil. The dignity of each one has been attacked. The emotional and moral growth of the victim has been thwarted. The innocence of the victim is disfigured. He or she can hope for and seek Christ's healing, but the optimal development toward healthy sexual integration within the context of deepest human dignity has been seriously damaged.

In light of this tragedy, the bishops and religious superiors have worked out guidelines and norms for reporting sexual abuse. We are now called to a new vigilance for the sake of the potential and actual victims. This entails a conversion of our own hearts to deeper insights into the dignity of each person who has been redeemed by Jesus Christ our Lord.

On the other hand, however, we must also consider the pastoral care of the perpetrators of these crimes. Men abuse children for a variety of reasons, reasons that are by no means fully understood. We cannot easily associate the problem with a particular background; the abusers come from all across the theological, philosophical, political, and cultural spectrums. Nevertheless, after establishing clear policies to protect the children, we need somehow to find ways to serve these broken men and their spiritual, psychological, and social needs.

Of course, many of them will end up in prison, but that does not prevent us from visiting them. Some will end up in psychiatric treatment. Most will become isolated from their parishes and brother priests. In that state, they will desperately need our help, and we must try to help them.

As a last resort, if they should refuse correction and conversion, we may have to treat them, as Jesus said, "as a Gentile and a tax collector" (Mt 18:17). He meant that we must treat them as we treat the unbelievers who are in need of conversion. They must become part of our mission, to the extent that this is possible.

This does not mean we must give these men so much time that we neglect our other duties. But it does mean that we must never cease praying for them, counseling them, and presenting them with the gospel of Jesus Christ. And we need not let our fear of scandal stop us from caring for these men any more than our Lord Jesus Christ was stopped from visiting the house of Matthew, where tax collectors and other sinners gathered.

Confronting Our Own Sexuality

As priests, we have a double calling. On one hand, the Christian exual ethic, based on the goodness of God's creation and its redemption from fallenness and sin by Jesus Christ, applies to us. No Christian is exempt from growing holy in the whole of life, including the area of sexuality. This is especially true within marriage, since the procreative and unitive elements of the sexual relationship exist within the holy context of matrimony. But single Christians as well must learn to grow in holiness and personal integrity.

We priests in the Roman rite, and many priests in the other rites, take vows of celibacy. Studies indicate that most priests appreciate the gift of celibacy and are happy within its demands. However, this general acceptance of the celibate state is still not without challenges, even for happy and peaceful celibates.

Though no priest may legitimately express his sexuality in genital ways, that does not mean that the issue of his sexuality is settled. Each priest must learn to integrate his sexuality into every aspect of his life. This includes dealing the right way with temptations and sexual sins, as well as enjoying the wonderful strengths of sexuality within the celibate life.

The healthy sublimation of sexuality into creative work and loving tenderness toward sinners is important. The integration of sexuality into prayer life—particularly through Confession, meditation, and self-knowledge—is a lifelong process. Just as other men go through stages in their psychological and sexual self-understanding, so do celibates. The joy is that the greater the integration of sexuality into the call to holiness, the greater the peace and effectiveness in the priest's life.

We priests need human support to accomplish such integration. Psychological insight is very useful, and consultation with psychological experts has helped many priests in the process of sexual integration. However, sexuality is not merely physical and psychological; it also requires a spiritual component, whether one is married or celibate. Also, psychology is frequently confused about sexuality, the spiritual life, and the meaning of human expression.

For these reasons, we need to seek out those psychologists who are capable of deep insight into the intricacies of sexual integration on a psychological level as well as a spiritual level. We priests can also help each other through our counseling, administration of the sacrament of Reconciliation, and friendships. We can offer each other support through struggles without slipping into a supportiveness for sexual misconduct. We can grow in that sexual integration which recognizes the respect due the sexual dimension of life and its influence on promoting one another's dignity before God our Creator and Redeemer.

In short, we priests can work through this present crisis and the sudden freeze it has brought us. On the other side is a springtime of hope for the Church. Our own souls and the souls in our care will be deeply affected by our approach to these problems, either for good or for bad. Let us endeavor to walk forward, confident in Christ Jesus that this is a wonderful springtime preparing for a new and glorious Christian millennium.

Fr. Mitchell C. Pacwa, S.J., is a program host and producer for the Eternal Word Network (EWTN), formerly a professor of biblical studies, and the author of Catholics and the New Age *and* Father, Forgive Me, for I Am Frustrated *(Servant).*

ELEVEN

What Do We Tell the Children?
A Catechetical Moment

Kristine L. Franklin

There are three news magazines on our coffee table. Each one of them features the clergy sex scandal on the front page. We hear about it on the radio and read about it in our small local paper. Our friends who watch TV tell us the topic is covered in the news day and night and has been a favorite subject of the talk show hosts. Our priests have mentioned it more than once from the pulpit. Our bishop wrote us all a letter.

For months now we've been treated to a daily menu of pedophilia, pederasty, homosexuality, felony child abuse, cover-up, corruption, lawsuits, jail sentences, allegations, depositions, defrockings, denials. Take your pick. It's all ugly. Sexual sin of an utterly depraved variety, on an unprecedented scale and seemingly ignored by Church leaders, has shaken the Catholic Church to its very foundations.

The revelations are numbing. Some days it feels as though we might never hear the end of it. What good can come of such reprehensible behavior? On first glance it may not be obvious, but the truth is, this is a perfect catechetical moment. We parents have work to do.

Certainly small children should be shielded from exposure to the topic of sexual abuse in the same way they should be shielded from the nature and content of pornography. With older kids, however, connected as they are to the larger culture, questions are certain to arise that must be addressed. As the primary educators of our children, we need to seize the moment. In the context of the current scandal we have an important opportunity to supply the answers that will inform and strengthen our kids' faith.

Some of my friends complain that their kids are never interested in talking about "Church stuff." Believe me, they're interested now. They're wondering about a lot of things. We need to be ready with the truth.

The Truth About Sin

If there is one gigantic lesson to be learned from the sex abuse scandal, it is this: Sin always and only destroys. It's time to rid ourselves of the dangerous and dishonest catechetical attitude that treats sin as though it were a boo-boo or a "bad choice" rather than the road to eternal death that it truly is. Our kids are hearing about crimes and cover-ups from the media. They need straight talk about sin from us.

Sexual crimes perpetrated against children are sins, not mistakes. Sin is what we do when we say no to God and yes to disobedience at any level. It starts venial and ends up mortal. Our kids have a right to this truth. We have before us a distinct opportunity to get back to basics regarding the age-old problem of sin and its effects on a person's soul.

Our children need to hear about sin. We need to use the word, define the term, call a spade a spade. Our kids are listening.

How could priests do such sickening, evil things? It's a good question. How does anyone descend into depravity? How does anyone go from a state of grace and friendship with God to a state of spiritual death?

The answer is easy: One unrepented, unconfessed sin at a time. Our kids need to understand the potential each of us has to travel down the same dark path as the sex offenders. It's easy to point the finger and condemn. It's a lot harder to see how we are vulnerable to the seduction of grave sin. It's important to help our kids understand the process, especially in the sexual realm.

They will be tempted, that much is certain. It's our job to help them know what to do when the time comes for action.

Mortal sin begins in the mind as an unrejected temptation, an impure thought that a person chooses to roll around in the mind in the same way a jawbreaker rolls around in the mouth. The thought leads to fantasy, the fantasy to consideration of the act fantasized. These impure thoughts, which are themselves sins of the mind, when unconfessed and uncontrolled, lead eventually to seeking out the occasion of sin—looking for trouble. And when a person looks for sin, he won't fail to find it.

By the time a person has committed mortal sin, his conscience has become weak and easy to ignore. The deadly sin may then become a deadly habit, and the person who permitted himself that first "harmless" taste of immorality may find himself a slave to his sin. All sins have the potential to enslave us, but sexual sin is especially binding, as we're seeing in the media reports about repeat offenders. We need to know our own weak areas. Our kids need to learn to know theirs.

It's imperative that we help our kids understand that upright, moral people don't wake up one day and say, "I think I'll find a child and commit some felonious acts." The way to mortal sin isn't a long drop off the cliff of morality. It's a slimy, slippery slope, and once a person approaches the bottom, it's hard to stop the slide.

We can point out to our kids that in the case of the few priests who sinned so gravely, temptations that started in the secret place of the mind were eventually transformed into sins that destroyed souls, ruined the lives of victims, and scandalized the faithful. This is a sobering lesson for all of us, kids and grown-ups alike. Sin is real, and if it goes unrepented, the result is ruin both in this life and, apart from repentance, in the life to come.

The Truth About Salvation

Some might argue that sin is a depressing topic, that we shouldn't burden kids with "old-fashioned gloom and doom" or try to scare them with the possibility of hell. That's bunk. We wouldn't be loving parents if we failed to tell our kids that drinking drain cleaner is a deadly act. We make them buckle up. We forbid them to smoke. We teach them to look both ways before crossing the street.

Most parents are good at teaching their children to avoid physical danger. We should be even more diligent about the care of their souls, because hell is forever. Our job is to lead our kids to eternal safety in heaven.

They need to know the danger of unbridled sin. And they need to know the remedy. Without a good grasp of sin and how it operates in our souls, our kids will have a difficult time understanding the enormity of our loving God's gifts of forgiveness and salvation, or the power of our greatest weapon—the sacraments.

When we talk to our kids about the current crisis in the Church, it is an excellent time to review the truths of the Christian gospel. The word "gospel" means "good news." We are sinners (the bad news), but Christ died so that our sins could be forgiven and our broken relationship with God could be restored (the good news).

Through the sacraments, God gives us his own divine life. He washes away our sins and gives us a new start. He gives us the power and courage to say no to sin, to grow in holiness, and to desire what is good. When we are weak, he breathes his own mighty strength into our souls. He helps us to love him more than we love ourselves and our desires.

Just as a car is made to run on the road, not on the bottom of a lake, we were made to live in a relationship of love with God, not in the filthy bog of rebellion. Through the sacraments, the forgiveness of sins and the power to live in obedience are made present to us here and now. By grace we are enabled to wrestle the alligator of temptation when it's newly hatched, rather than waiting until it's twelve feet long.

Kids have an innate sense of justice. It may be difficult for them to understand that forgiveness of sins extends to the worst offenders. It's easy to imagine that God forgives little white lies or cuss words; it's harder to grasp the wideness of God's mercy with regard to grave and scandalous sins. Yet it is vital that we help our kids understand that the only mortal sin that can't be forgiven is an unrepented, unconfessed one.

They need to hear it from our lips: "No matter what a person does, no matter how terrible, if he is sincerely sorry and goes to Confession, Jesus is waiting with open arms to forgive and heal." Sin is a deadly disease. Jesus is the Doctor whose cure always works, even when the sins are heinous. That's why the Good News is so good!

The Truth About Our Church

In order to guarantee that the gospel message would be preserved and preached until the end of time, and that the life-giving sacraments would be available in every generation, Jesus established the Catholic Church. He promised that nothing, not even Satan himself, would ever bring down the Church. This is an awesome and reassuring truth, especially in a time of crisis. In more than two thousand years of history the Catholic Church has withstood heresy, division, rebellion, persecution, oppression, and every kind of scandal imaginable. We need to remind our kids of this fact.

The Church is made up of sinners who sometimes fail miserably, but it is still the Church of Jesus Christ, protected by his promise and the power of the Holy Spirit. Its teachings will always be trustworthy, and its sacraments will continue to extend the grace of God to those who accept it.

It may be hard for kids to understand that the Church remains stable and trustworthy despite the sinfulness of some of its ministers. We can point out that because God chooses priests and bishops from among sinners (all of us!), there will always be some priests and bishops who are not faithful to their vows. This is a sad fact of life. It was true when Jesus chose the Apostles, it has been true all through Church history, and it is true now.

Sinful priests do not take away from the truth of the message of salvation, nor do they invalidate the sacraments. If anything, they demonstrate the universal need for mercy and grace. The Church survives despite the sinfulness of its members, and it will survive until Christ comes again in glory. Our kids need to be reassured of this truth.

The Truth About Hope

Judas collected his money and betrayed Jesus with a kiss, and suddenly everything Jesus had worked to build was destroyed. At least, that's how it looked to the first disciples. But now we know the rest of the story: From betrayal, injustice, torture, and death, God brought us salvation through his Son, Jesus Christ.

The worst thing in the world turned into the best thing in the universe. God can bring good out of the present situation, too. We need to help our kids affirm this hope.

What good can God bring from the sex abuse scandal? We should ask our kids this question, help them think out loud. If God can use the scandal of the cross to bring redemption to the world, what might he do in the aftermath of this tragedy? Here are some conclusions we reached at our house.

- Priests who have done bad things will be punished.
- Bishops will be more picky about who gets to be a priest, and maybe the Pope will get more picky about who can be a bishop.
- People will pray for priests more.
- Priests who are involved in sexual sin will get a wake-up call.
- Priests who want to be holy will try even harder.
- People who are angry will have to forgive.
- We'll get better at defending our faith.
- People will know that the Catholic Church is true because something terrible like this can't knock it down.

Perhaps your children, like mine, will teach you a few things, too.

We are sinners. We need the Savior. We need his grace, his power, his forgiveness, and most of all, his love.

We need humility. We need to recognize our own vulnerable areas. We need to keep our minds pure. We need to avoid the circumstances that entice us to give in to sin. We need to pray for courage, and we need to receive the sacraments often. What great lessons for every one of us!

This life is not a party. It's a battle, and our soul is the prize. Each of us is called to be a saint. We are weak, but he is strong. If our kids come away from this situation with a deeper understanding of the seriousness of sin and the power of salvation, much good will come of this sorrowful but catechetical moment in history.

Kristine L. Franklin is the award-winning author of twelve books for children and young adults. She has cohosted two series for Eternal Word Television Network and is a popular conference speaker and a frequent contributor to several Catholic publications. Kristine and her husband, Marty, are the parents of two children.

TWELVE

The View From Outside
What Do We Say to Non-Catholics About the Scandals?

Al Kresta

To be angry is easy, but to be angry at the right men, at the right time, for the right reason, is difficult." So the ancient Greek hero Odysseus taught his son, Telemachus, as they reclaimed Odysseus' home from the sordid suitors who had abused his wife and dishonored his memory during his long absence.

While the "anger of man does not work the righteousness of God" (Jas 1:20), we are sometimes visited by a divine discontent and fury that flash through human beings in a blaze of prophecy. The present crisis caused by clerical sexual abuse and episcopal negligence affords one such time for anger. Here we see not merely pathetic human brokenness, but the horror of human evil. Here growls not the anger of man, but the wrath of God.

In the sweep of this righteous indignation, the moneychangers in the temple find their true identity. Here the perverts in the Catholic priesthood find their true names: false shepherds and wolves in sheep's clothing (see Mt 7:15-17). Moral outrage is a necessary and proper response of Catholics and non-Catholics alike in this situation because it calls sin by its name.

Thus the first thing to keep in mind when Catholics discuss the subject with non-Catholics is that we shouldn't hesitate to express our anger. Such outrage, in fact, forms a healthy and natural common ground for all people with even the most basic of moral sensitivities. Non-Catholics need to know that we are as offended by these crimes as they are.

A Gracious Response From Non-Catholics

Most serious non-Catholics with whom I've conversed on this topic have demonstrated magnanimity and grace, even while serious Catholics rage. They often refrain from bringing up the matter out of respect for the many good works of the Catholic Church. The Lutheran philosopher Gilbert Meilander, for instance, before exploring the subject with me, first mentioned the problems his own tradition has in shifting divorced pastors from parish to parish.

Evangelical Protestant leader Chuck Colson gracefully acknowledged his lack of jurisdiction in a recent statement: "Failure to respond to this information has many Catholics, like my friend Bill Bennett, calling for Cardinal Law's resignation. As I've previously stated, as a Baptist, I leave that to my Roman Catholic friends to decide."

Thoughtful people of other religious faiths also know that men and women in their own traditions are vulnerable to the charge of sexual misconduct. The memory of Jim Bakker and of Jimmy Swaggart hasn't faded. And there are plenty of local examples. Here in Michigan, for instance, we had a Christian and Missionary Alliance pastor from Detroit convicted of a few bank robberies that he carried out to fuel his pornography habit.

The recent "Candyman" Internet child porn sting, you may recall, included eight clergymen. Only two of them were Catholic priests. What were the ecclesiastical affiliations of the others?

Our evangelical friends in particular know the reality of human sin and the redemption that is available in Christ. Their leaders, generally, don't take any delight in lampooning the leadership of the Catholic Church. They know that Jesus had his Judas, and that you don't judge a community by those who don't live out the faith but by those who do.

Anti-Catholics and "Dissenting" Catholics

On the other hand, we must distinguish anti-Catholics from non-Catholics. Anti-Catholics refuse to acknowledge the Catholic Church as a legitimate Christian tradition and regard membership within her ranks as a diabolical participation in the spirit of anti-Christ. Not surprisingly, anti-Catholics have exploited this crisis as a golden moment to call people out of the Church.

Few, I'm thankful to say, are leaving as a result of the scandal. A recent national poll reported that 3 percent of Catholics are reexamining their relationship with the Catholic Church. This makes me chuckle. I would think that at any given moment at least that many Catholics are reconsidering their commitment to the Church. The percentage claimed is actually lower than the margin of error for the poll.

In any case, reasoned conversation with sheep-stealing anti-Catholics regarding the current scandal is probably impossible and would lead to mere quarrels rather than dialogue, discussion, or edifying argument.

We must note as well the self-loathing Catholics who are using this situation as an opportunity either to blame Church leadership for their own spiritual mediocrity or to attempt to justify their theological dissent. Groups such as "Call to Action" have purchased billboard space calling for the ordination of women. I'm still trying to figure out how the ordination of women will keep certain men who vowed celibacy from chasing teenage boys. We should also keep in mind recent reports that nuns have also been guilty of committing sexual crimes against children.

So let me be clear. This problem did not come about through the failure of the Catholic tradition. It came about because ordained leadership has failed to live faithfully according to the Tradition. That reality is one we should emphasize in conversations with anti-Catholics and "dissenting" Catholics alike.

Issues to Discuss

In thoughtful discussion with non-Catholics who are seeking a better understanding of the situation, I think we should talk about several important issues.

Holding Bishops Responsible

First, faithful Catholics need to let their non-Catholic acquaintances know that we do not intend to let our bishops off the hook. Respect for our bishops means telling them the truth and holding them to the truth.

Bishop Carl Mengeling of the diocese of Lansing, Michigan, put it this way: "We have to be aware of the horror of the betrayal of trust by some priests and bishops. That awareness of the crime and sin has to be *burned* into the minds of the leadership of the Church."

George Orwell, author of *1984* and *Animal Farm,* once wrote that he lived in an age when stating the obvious was the first duty of an intelligent man. To my non-Catholic friends, I must state the obvious, because many American bishops have failed to do so: Those who have sinned must repent, believe the gospel, and make restitution. There is no justification for these crimes, immoral acts, or abuses of office.

The limp apologies we have heard do not ultimately satisfy. We want explanations and accountability, not excuses. How did leadership come to tolerate or create an ecclesiastical culture in which a Shanley, a Geoghan, a Kos, a Porter, and a Gauthe could operate for years?

According to the gospel, sin must not be excused merely as a mistake, shortcoming, or disease. We must do something much more difficult. We must forgive it. But forgiveness is not flabby. It is costly. And I'm not talking about some diocesan dollars tossed out as settlements.

The gospel is good news, but reconciliation may also require that we make restitution and seek to repair the damage our sin has caused. Grace is not cheap. There are temporal consequences of our sins that must be borne—borne, we would hope, in imitation of Christ—by the guilty parties. We must try to undo the damage our sin has caused to others. As faithful Catholics, we expect such restitution to be made to help restore some balance to the moral order of the world.

Mitigating Circumstances

I have no interest in muting the moral outrage or making excuses for the behavior of our clergy. But in defense of the Church, there are a few important mitigating circumstances that should be clarified in our discussions with non-Catholics.

Priests are no more likely to abuse than other clergymen. Philip Jenkins, Penn State University professor of history and religious studies, is the author of *Pedophiles and Priests: Anatomy of a Contemporary Crisis* (Oxford, 1996). In personal conversation and in public sessions, Jenkins has over and over made the point: "There is no evidence that the rate of sexual abuse and misconduct among Catholic clergy is any higher than the rate among clergy of non-Catholic Christian denominations; or among clergy of non-Christian religions, or for non-clergy professions involved with children, such as teachers and scoutmasters."[1]

The best study we have of this matter involved twenty-two hundred Chicago-area priests. Approximately 1.8 percent had been involved in sexual misconduct with minors. Pedophiles—that is, those who engaged in sex with pre-pubescent children—were a tiny fraction of 1 percent. This deviant percentage of priests has brought discredit on the vast number of faithful clergy who have made sacrificial commitments to follow Christ and serve others.

Church leaders were influenced in the past by earlier social attitudes and professional medical advice. Between about 1950 and 1977, mainstream professional opinion did not regard child sexual molestation as especially dangerous. Concern over child sexual abuse was in some ways an outgrowth of feminist concern over "father rape" and began growing as an issue in the mid-1970s. Jenkins reports that between 1976 and 1986, the number of reports of child abuse and neglect in the United States rose from 669,000 to more than 2,000,000.

Medical views on the criminality and treatability of these problems have changed over the years. This change needs to be considered when indicting Church leadership for what often seems a too-forgiving approach to the problem of erring clergy.

Media attempts to keep the public debate politically correct have confused the issues. The current scandals rarely involve pedophilia, that is, sex with pre-pubescent children. They are mostly about homosexual desire toward young men. The vast majority of recorded instances of clergy sexual misconduct involve an interest in teenagers of either gender, often boys of fifteen or sixteen.

Just carefully read the reports, do the math on the ages, and ask, "Why isn't the press reporting this as a homosexual issue?" This silence is especially galling because homosexual novels, documentaries, and first-person testimonies are rife with rites of initiation and passage in which an older man seduces a younger man, helping him to "realize his true sexual self" and homosexual inclination. We might reasonably charge the media with hypocrisy here: They have treated the Boy Scouts harshly for doing what the Catholic Church failed to do.

The media have done the Church a service by bringing this matter to light, but they have not always been fair or accurate in their treatment of the crisis. Just as God used the pagan Assyrians and Babylonians to judge ancient Israel, so too he has used the media to force the Catholic faithful to deal with this problem. Yet even though we might commend the *Boston Globe* for intrepid reporting, we must also remember that the secular press is no more a friend of God's covenant people than were the Assyrians and the Babylonians.

The Catholic Church, because of its institutional unity, its role as the largest nongovernmental organization in America, and the "mystique" of clerical celibacy, is most commonly referenced in press accounts of clergy sexual misconduct. That lends a prominence to Catholic clergy dalliances that other Christian traditions luckily escape. For instance, CBS News.com reported on March 19, 2002:

"The FBI says it expects to arrest at least fifty more people by week's end as it busts up an Internet child-pornography ring that allegedly included two Catholic priests, six other members of the clergy, a school bus driver, and at least one police officer."

I am not interested in bringing discredit upon Presbyterians, Methodists, Lutherans, or Episcopalians. But why was it that among the eight clergy only Catholic priests were referenced? It was because the media is treating this as an institutional problem of the Church rather than an individual problem of particular priests, even though there is no evidence that the problem is greater among Catholic clergy than other clergy or professionals working with children.

Along with the important reporting that has occurred, there is also a feeding frenzy that fails to make crucial distinctions between the journalistic pieces of red meat thrown in the trough. Not all instances of misconduct are instances of sexual abuse! For example, the recent resignation of Archbishop Rembert Weakland of Milwaukee occurred amid accusations of "sexual abuse" and "sexual assault." But the truth is that the person he allegedly "abused" or "assaulted" was thirty-three years old at the time, and this particular situation had all the makings of a consensual homosexual relationship.

Nevertheless, in the current climate the press is not distinguishing between pedophilia, sexual misconduct with minors, heterosexual sex, or homosexual sex. All is reduced to sexual "abuse," even when the story is really about abuse of office or violation of vows.

Celibacy is not the problem. Among some non-Catholics I've talked to, I've noticed a suspicion that celibacy is unnatural. The truth is that celibacy is not natural or unnatural. It is supernatural. It is a distinct gift given by God to certain individuals so they may more ardently serve the kingdom of God. Both Jesus and St. Paul considered celibacy a benefit for the kingdom, not a liability (see Mt 19:10-12; 1 Cor 7:7-8, 28, 32-35).

It is true that some priests of the last generation entered the seminary thinking that the discipline of celibacy would be changed. Others had a distorted understanding of their vow. I know of one priest who said: "I took a vow not to marry. I didn't vow not to have sex." It is difficult to understand how such a man could be ordained.

Nevertheless, the issue of celibacy is ultimately a red herring. Who wants to abolish the vow of marital fidelity because some husbands and wives commit adultery? Does anybody really think that by allowing priests to marry we will keep them from seducing fourteen-year-old boys?

The seal of the confessional must be maintained. Occasionally a non-Catholic friend will argue that a priest should turn over to the civil authorities information gained in the sacrament of Reconciliation if that information will further the safety of young children. The issue has in fact recently been debated in the Connecticut state legislature, where an attempt was made to pass a law requiring such disclosures. So it is important to think this issue through.

The canon law of the Church explicitly forbids such a violation of confidentiality. The seal of the confessional is a recognition that the God to whom we confess our sins in the sacrament is supreme. He is our ultimate sanctuary, even for the criminal.

There are simply some places where Caesar is not Lord, even if we believe in a highly centralized state. A priest may ask the penitent to confess to the civil authorities as a condition of receiving absolution. But we must leave that to the pastoral discretion of the clergy.

Information about criminal activity gained outside the confessional is a different story, of course, and the laws governing these kinds of clergy conversations vary from state to state.

The antidote to this objection is probably best found in watching Alfred Hitchcock's 1953 film *I Confess,* starring Montgomery Clift as the embattled priest in a murder trial. This film sensitively explores the issues arising when the seal of the confessional seems to come in conflict with the state's need for criminal evidence.

The Church has survived much worse crises, and it will survive this one. Finally, we must help non-Catholics realize that the Catholic Church thinks in terms of centuries, and it has centuries of experience behind it. We've been through this before. Perhaps the most scandalous pope in history, Alexander VI, had nine children from six different concubines. But he was so busy sinning that he never got around to doing much teaching. His personal sin, though it caused grave public scandal, did not ruin the Church.

When Francis of Assisi was asked what he would do if he knew that a priest celebrating Mass had concubines, he said: "When it came time for Holy Communion, I would go to receive the sacred Body of my Lord from the priest's anointed hands." The sacraments are not the work of man, but of God.

Whether the bread and wine are consecrated by St. Augustine or by a priest on death row for rape and murder, it is Christ himself who acts to give us his own Body and Blood. Ultimately, our faith is in him, not in the moral integrity of individual clergymen. If, as Jesus promised, the gates of hell won't prevail against the Church (see Mt 16:17-19), a few perverse priests and negligent bishops certainly won't.

✦

Al Kresta is CEO of Ave Maria Communications and host of a syndicated three-hour daily radio talk show, "Kresta in the Afternoon." He is also a founding member of Catholics for Authentic Reform (online, go to www.petersvoice.com/catholicreform/), a group formed in response to the current crisis.

---

1. See Philip Jenkins, *Pedophiles and Priests: Anatomy of a Contemporary Crisis* (New York: Oxford, 1996). The quote is from a personal conversation between Jenkins and the author.

THIRTEEN

Don't Get Mad; Get Holy
Overcoming Evil With Good

Leon Suprenant

T he current clerical sex abuse scandal is a tragedy that has sent shock waves through the Catholic Church and American society. Catholic dioceses face many pastoral and legal challenges as they address the needs of victims while also developing policies to prevent such crimes from occurring in the future. Surely, as Pope John Paul II says, "The abuse which has caused this crisis is by every standard wrong and rightly considered a crime by society; it is also an appalling sin in the eyes of God."[1]

This scandal has caused harm to the entire Church. Most obviously, there are the victims of the sex abuse themselves and their families, who so much need healing and love. The perpetrators of these crimes have caused tremendous physical and spiritual harm (see Mt 18:6-9) and have dire need of divine mercy, in addition to medical treatment and criminal sanction. There are the many good and faithful priests and religious who suddenly find themselves the objects of suspicion, hatred, and perhaps even false charges. And then there is the larger Church, whose pastoral and missionary efforts have been compromised by the sins of a few of her members.

In addition to all this pain, there is also the considerable anger, frustration, betrayal, sadness, confusion, and outrage experienced by Catholics and non-Catholics alike over this crisis. These feelings are directed not only toward the perpetrators of these crimes but also toward a Church bureaucracy and ecclesial climate that would allow repeat offenders to remain in active ministry. The Holy Father affirms that "because of the great harm done by some priests and religious, the Church herself is viewed with distrust, and many are offended at the way in which the Church's leaders are perceived to have acted in this matter."[2]

Further, many faithful Catholics are profoundly offended when the Church is unfairly vilified in the media and when opponents and critics of the Church capitalize on this opportunity to attack the Church and promote their own agendas in the process.

This position paper does not attempt to provide a comprehensive treatment of the spiritual, psychological, and sociological dimensions of this problem, nor does it examine the intra-ecclesial procedures that are being put in place to more effectively address claims of clerical misconduct in the future.

Rather, as a private association of lay Catholics, Catholics United for the Faith (CUF) desires in this position paper to provide sound, practical guidance to lay Catholics who desire to be faithful to Jesus Christ and his Church, notwithstanding the scandalous behavior of some of her members.

The size and gravity of the current clerical sex abuse scandal can lead to anger, discouragement, and a sense of powerlessness. Yet our Lord promised to be with us until the end of the world, and he can—and does—bring about good from even the greatest evils when we put our trust in him (see Rom 8:28). In point of fact, there are many things we can do to be "part of the solution," to cooperate with divine grace to make a difference in this crisis. Therefore, we offer the following eight practical steps Catholic laity can take to help bring some good out of this unspeakable evil.

Holiness

In every age, and particularly during times of crisis, what the Church needs most is saints—the example and intercession of holy men and women. "The saints have always been the source and origin of renewal in the most difficult moments in the Church's history" (*CCC* 828). In our time we've been blessed with Pope John Paul II and Mother Teresa—both celibates—whose holy lives bear effective, credible witness to the gospel they proclaim.

But as Vatican II teaches, holiness is not just for Catholic "superstars" like the Pope but also for rank-and-file lay Catholics. Therefore, the first order of business must be a renewal of our own commitment to the Lord and his body, the Church. We must commit ourselves to daily prayer and the sacramental life of the Church as the first—not last—resort.

Not without reason does our Lord counsel us to remove the planks from our own eyes before trying to remove splinters from others' eyes (see Mt 7:3). Imagine there's a mishap on an airplane, and the craft begins losing cabin pressure. In the face of such a calamity, most of us would want to be courageous, to do the right thing and help as many of our fellow passengers as possible. Yet if we don't use our own air mask first, in a matter of seconds we'll be of no use to anybody. We would be among the first casualties.

While there may be other righteous actions we can take, if we were only to devote ourselves to prayer, frequent reception of the sacraments of Confession and Holy Communion, weekly if not daily holy hours of reparation before the Blessed Sacrament, spiritual and corporal works of mercy, and other such activities out of love for our Lord and a desire to help rebuild his Church, we would be providing the greatest service we can possibly give.

Faith

We should pray specifically for an increase of the virtue of faith (see Lk 17:5). That language may be off-putting to some. After all, we either have faith or we don't, right? Yet we surely need to believe all that God has revealed through Christ and his Church with greater understanding, conviction, and joy.

Even more, the virtue of faith enables us to see the fullness of reality, with its natural and supernatural components. Faith enables us to see the divine amid the human. Jesus is not simply a good man but the Second Person of the Blessed Trinity. Scripture is not just a collection of ancient human writings but also truly the work of the Holy Spirit. And the Church is not simply a human "institution" but also the Mystical Body of Christ and the means of salvation for the whole world.

It takes a strong faith to acknowledge an "apostolic" Church if the "apostle" in our midst fails in his duties. It takes a strong faith to accept a "holy" Church when we're constantly having the sins of her members—and even some of her leaders—rubbed in our faces.

We cannot deny the shortcomings and failures of members of the Church through the ages, including those that have been publicized in recent months. But we do need the virtue of faith to see the greater reality. The best way to grow in faith is to ask the Lord for this gift. Here is one popular Act of Faith that can be used to ask the Lord to increase our faith:

O my God, I firmly believe that you are one God in three divine Persons, Father, Son, and Holy Spirit. I believe that your divine Son became man and died for our sins, and that he will come to judge the living and the dead. I believe these and all the truths which the holy Catholic Church teaches, because you have revealed them, who can neither deceive nor be deceived. Amen.

Vocations

Vatican II clearly called upon all the faithful to beg the Lord of the harvest for more laborers in the vineyard (see Mt 9:36-38), particularly for an increase of vocations to the priesthood and religious life. In a special way, this call goes out to families, which must be "incubators" of vocations in the Church (see *CCC* 1656). Parents must not exert pressure on their children when it comes to choosing a state in life, but rather they should encourage their children to follow Jesus and to accept with generosity whatever specific vocation the Lord has in store for them (see *CCC* 2230, 2232).

Sadly, some parents do not want their children to become priests or religious. Yet the *Catechism* teaches: "Parents should welcome and respect with joy and thanksgiving the Lord's call to one of their children to follow him in virginity for the sake of the Kingdom in the consecrated life or in priestly ministry" (*CCC* 2233).

If, however, our focus is only on the next generation of priests, then we're missing an increasingly significant aspect of our vocations effort. Many priests and religious feel the spiritual and material support of the faithful while they're in formation, but then they are ordained or take their final vows and seemingly fall off the intercessory map. More than ever, all priests and religious need the prayers, support, and encouragement of all the Church.

In times past, a parish might have had three or four priests in residence. Now often there is just one, and increasingly he is serving two or more parishes. Further, with the latest scandals, all priests more than ever are the butt of jokes and subjected to derision and anti-Catholic venom. The Lord surely will bless efforts to support our beloved priests through our prayers and our friendship (see Mt 10:40-42).

Church Support

Catholics have the duty of providing for the material needs of the Church, each according to his abilities (see *CCC* 2043; Code of Canon Law, canon 222). This can be a real stumbling block for some Catholics today, especially in dioceses where millions of dollars are being paid to settle sex abuse lawsuits.

First, it should be understood that funds donated in the weekly collection plate or to an annual diocesan campaign are not typically the source of the funds used when the diocese settles a lawsuit. Even so, the diocese should spell this out specifically for the faithful so that there is no misunderstanding as to how the settlements are being funded. Clearly, the Church's immense humanitarian, educational, parochial, and missionary activities are dependent upon the ongoing support of Catholics.

Even more, we must learn from the account of the widow's mite (see Lk 21:1-4). Her contribution was inconsequential, but she was held up for special praise because she gave what she had, not simply what she could spare.

In the Old Testament, our Lord accuses those who refuse to tithe of stealing from him (see Mal 3:8). Surely lay people have the right to decide to which parishes, diocesan programs, religious communities, and apostolates they will contribute, and they will likely contribute their hard-earned money to those entities that they consider to be the best stewards of their offerings. But our Lord and his Church are clear about our need to do what we can to support the Church.

"Generosity" literally means "full of giving life." Putting our time, talent, and treasure at the service of the Church is a reflection of the priority of Jesus Christ in our lives (see Mt 6:24) and will help breathe new life into the Church in the new millennium.

Avoid Scandal

We have to be so careful today in terms of how we talk about the priesthood and contemporary issues facing the Church. Probably the harshest critics of the Church are former Catholics and those who still consider themselves Catholic but who oppose the Church on any number of issues.

It's very easy to find fault in the Church right now. People are rightly upset and disturbed. When we give verbal expression to these feelings, we may be just "letting off steam," and everything we say may well be true. But having part of the truth and needing to let off steam do not excuse making statements that will harm the faith of other Catholics whose faith perhaps is weaker, provide an unnecessary stumbling block for nonbelievers, and needlessly and perhaps even unfairly harm the reputations of others (see *CCC* 2477).

In place of the above, Scripture is very clear. We are told to say "only the things men need to hear, things that will help them" (see Eph 4:29). As St. Paul says, "Whatever is true, whatever is honorable, whatever is just, whatever is pure, whatever is lovely, whatever is gracious, if there is any excellence, if there is anything worthy of praise, think about these things" (Phil 4:8).

Scandal involves inducing others to sin (see *CCC* 2284-87). It's a type of spiritual murder. Are our comments regarding the Church being expressed in ways that will actually turn people against the Church? And if *giving* scandal is like spiritual murder, then *taking* scandal is akin to spiritual suicide. We must protect our own hearts, that we do not allow our own negative feelings about the real evils in some dioceses to fester and ultimately to lead us out of the Church.

In the business world there's a maxim that may help us take the right approach in this matter. Successful managers are able to "catch their employees doing something right" and in the process provide positive reinforcement for good behavior. In the spiritual realm, we likewise do well to "overcome evil with good" (Rom 12:21).

There are holy people in the Church. There are many great stories of contemporary Christian heroes, not to mention the lives of saints through the centuries. There is much good going on in the Church on many different fronts, globally, nationally, and in our backyard. We need to acknowledge and publicize this truth.

This does not mean that we ignore the sins of Church members. As we discussed above, the Church is at once holy yet always in need of renewal and reform, and *charitably* correcting a sinner is a spiritual work of mercy.

Using an analogy, let us assume that a husband and wife are having marital problems, and the husband wants to do something about it. The first step would be for the husband honestly to acknowledge the nature and extent of the problem. He would try to work things out with his spouse, and no one would criticize him for seeking the help of others—marital counselors, spiritual advisors, friends and confidantes, and above all God himself—to help remedy the problem.

However, if the husband were to begin to vilify his wife to his children, to neighbors, perhaps even to the press, we can say that regardless of the truth and frustration level behind his statements, he would only be hurting the situation. Notice that St. Joseph, when confronted with the apparent infidelity of his wife, determined to "divorce her *quietly*," without subjecting her to shame (see Mt 1:19). As Catholics, we similarly have to distinguish acknowledging the truth and taking restorative action from mere venting and causing greater division within the Church.

Engaging the World

The Holy Father has continually called for a "new evangelization" or a reevangelization of formerly Christian cultures. We should not confuse "new evangelization" with "easy evangelization," nor should we expect the seeds of a "new springtime of faith" to sprout without opposition, persecution, and indeed, the blood of martyrs.

An integral part of the new evangelization entails a prudent engagement with the world. Catholic laity need to be holy, and they need to be informed. The Catholic Church is frequently battered in the media. We can't run from the media, but neither should we accept the media's rules of engagement—rules that often preclude, among other things, the existence of God and an objective moral law. We need, with God's grace, to be smarter and more convincing, not more fearful, compromising, or inflammatory.

And all of us know people, many of whom were raised Catholic, who have an inadequate understanding of the Christian faith generally and who are inclined to accept uncritically whatever evil the media attributes to the Church. Being able to put such attacks in their proper light is an important form of apologetics, of being prepared to make a defense, with gentleness and reverence, of the abiding hope that is in us (see 1 Pt 3:15).

Bishops

Both the enemies of the Church and many of those who wish to come to her defense tend to blame the bishops for any and all evils in the Church. Certainly the bishop is responsible for his particular church, or diocese, and throughout Church history, including in the present time, there have been bishops who have not been faithful to the sacred office entrusted to them. When such infidelity or malfeasance occurs, the Church suffers greatly.

Yet it is futile to envision a Church without bishops, as they are legitimate successors of the apostles who bear the authority of Christ (see *CCC* 800, 886, 888). They are spiritual fathers in the Church.[3]

One important teaching of Vatican II, which has also found its way into the current Code of Canon Law, is the laity's right to bring their concerns respectfully to their bishops (see *CCC* 907). Such a right should be exercised in a constructive way and not simply as a justification to attack or condemn. The faithful should encourage their bishops to take appropriate action not only in clerical sex abuse cases, but also in related issues to the extent they are relevant, such as seminary screening, ministry to homosexuals, classroom sex education in Catholic schools, and other such issues.

Ambassadors of Reconciliation

Regardless of our state in life, all of us as Christ's disciples are called to be ambassadors of his reconciliation, mercy, and healing:

> All this is from God, who through Christ reconciled us to himself and gave us the ministry of reconciliation; that is, in Christ God was reconciling the world to himself, not counting their trespasses against them, and entrusting to us the message of reconciliation. So we are ambassadors for Christ, God making his appeal through us. We beseech you on behalf of Christ, be reconciled to God.
>
> 2 CORINTHIANS 5:18-20

A lively sense of divine mercy is so needed today, and we need to be its instruments as well as its recipients. We must be ambassadors of reconciliation within the Church, afflicted as she is with dissent and scandal. Without in any way minimizing the need to bring criminals to justice, we need to forgive from the heart the perpetrators of the crimes that have been committed as well as those who have allowed such crimes to continue, all the while praying for their repentance and conversion.

We must be instruments of the Lord's healing and compassion to all those who have been directly harmed by abusive priests. We must repeatedly forgive those who have used the scandal as a pretext for attacking the Church and for furthering their own agendas, even as we peaceably answer their charges. And we need to be instruments of God's mercy and peace to all those we meet.

The current situation does not need more heat. Rather, it needs the light of Christ. May we be ambassadors of the light of Christ to a society that is frequently walking in darkness (see Mt 4:12-17; 5:14-16).

In this time of tribulation, when there are such grievous wounds inflicted on the body of Christ, we must pray much more fervently for the Church, for all victims, for our bishops, priests, and seminarians, that this great suffering may be for the purification of the Church and that the necessary exposure of evil may have a medicinal effect. This should be a wake-up call also for each of us poor sinners. We too are at fault because of our lukewarmness.

We must do penance and make reparation for the offense against God. We already can see that Christ in his mercy is in the process of purifying his Bride the Church. We must pray unceasingly that Christ will have the final victory. This is the sentiment of our beloved Holy Father, who has said:

We must be confident that this time of trial will bring a purification of the entire Catholic community, a purification that is urgently needed if the Church is to preach more effectively the Gospel of Jesus Christ in all its liberating force. Now you must ensure that where sin increased, grace will all the more abound (see Rom 5:20). So much pain, so much sorrow must lead to a holier priesthood, a holier episcopate, a holier Church.

God alone is the source of holiness, and it is to him above all that we must turn for forgiveness, for healing, and for the grace to meet this challenge with uncompromising courage and harmony of purpose.[4]

∴⁎∴

Leon Suprenant is the president of Catholics United for the Faith and Emmaus Road Publishing, as well as publisher of Lay Witness, an award-winning magazine for lay Catholics. He is general editor with Scott Hahn of the best-selling book Catholic for a Reason: Scripture and the Mystery of the Family of God *(Emmaus Road). This essay is an excerpt from the "Position Paper of Catholics United for the Faith on the Current Clerical Sex Abuse Scandal," copyright 2002, Catholics United for the Faith. Used with permission. For the complete text of the position paper, go to www.cuf.org/apr02a.htm, or call 800-693-2484 for a free copy.*

1. See "Address of Pope John Paul II to the Cardinals of the United States and Conference Officers," on pp. 209-2011 of this book.

2. See "Address," p. 209.

3. For a more complete treatment of this subject, see *Servants of the Gospel* (Emmaus Road Publishing, 1999; call 800-398-5470), a collection of essays by U.S. bishops on the role of the bishop in the Church today, as well as Catholics United for the Faith's FAITH FACT "Following Our Bishops" (call 1-800-MY-FAITH or visit www.cuf.org), which summarizes Church teaching on the subject so as to foster an "open-eyed obedience"—neither "blind obedience" nor wide-eyed defiance.

4. "Address," p. 209.

FOURTEEN

"I, Eternal Truth, Promise to Refresh You"
From Long Ago, God's Words of Hope for Today

Paul Thigpen

The Church is in turmoil. Reports of clerical misconduct scandalize the public. From every quarter come stories of priests having sex with men and sex with women, fathering children, refusing to preach against immorality, engaging in heterodox ceremonies alien to the Christian faith.

The behavior of some bishops is equally scandalous. They fail to correct the priests under their oversight, either through a misguided sense of mercy or because they themselves are morally compromised. They seem to display no fear of God. They misuse Church funds. They are arrogantly out of touch with their flocks and seem to care little for the welfare of the victims of clerical abuse. They hanker after status and promotion within the hierarchy, and their worldliness keeps their attention focused more on temporal concerns than spiritual ones.

Does this seem a reasonable summary of certain problems facing the Catholic Church in America in the spring of 2002? Think again. I am actually describing the predicament of the Catholic Church in Italy more than six hundred years ago, in the fall of 1377.

How do we know about these dismal conditions so long ago? In the

Dialogue of St. Catherine of Siena (1347-1380), we find a record of this remarkable woman's extended conversations with God. She provides us there a startling, even outrageous portrait of a Church in desperate need of reform, much like the Church of our day.

Our Times Are Not Unique

Why should it make any difference to us that St. Catherine's time was so much like our own? First, her account of medieval scandal should comfort us by reminding us that our dismaying situation is by no means historically unique. This is no doubt a cold comfort, but it has its uses; misery loves company. The truth is that evidence from many historical periods suggests that problems of sexual sin among the clergy and religious are perennial in Church history.

In the early centuries of the Church, for example, homosexual activity and even sexual abuse of children were apparently common enough among the ancient monks that monastic leaders had to account for it in the governance of their communities. St. Basil warned that handsome younger monks must keep their attractiveness cloaked to avoid arousing lust in the older monks. Abba Macarius and Abba Isaac, desert fathers in Egypt, rebuked the monastic communities that accepted boys into their midst and lamented the resulting pederasty that brought spiritual ruin. St. Benedict's rule had to insist that when monks slept in the same room, they must sleep in separate beds, with a lamp burning all night and with the elderly men distributed between the younger ones.

In the early Middle Ages, a regional Church council in seventh-century Spain found it necessary to decree that clergymen convicted of homosexual behavior would be degraded from Holy Orders and exiled. The ninth-century emperor Charlemagne rebuked the clergy and religious of his day for permitting homosexual sin to flourish within the monasteries. St. Peter Damian, an eleventh-century Church reformer, was outraged by the widespread practice of homosexual priests confessing to each other to avoid being discovered and to receive mild penances. Clerical spiritual advisors, too, he complained, often had sex with those under their care.

In the later Middle Ages we have, not only St. Catherine's report, but also the eleventh-century testimony of the great reformer St. Bernard of Clairvaux. He compared the Church of his day to a resurrected version of Sodom and Gomorrah. The ashes of those divinely incinerated cities were scattered throughout the clergy, he insisted. The "poisonous offspring" of those "cities of vice" boldly committed homosexual sin and then offered the Blessed Sacrament with defiled hands and hearts.

In the Renaissance, we need only note Pope Alexander VI, the notorious prelate belonging to the infamous Borgia family. As a cardinal he sired children by several women; one of his sons he arranged to be made a bishop at the age of seven. As pope he added several more women to his list of concubines and fathered more children by them. Nor did he attempt to hide his sins: He paraded his offspring openly, lavishing gifts and honors on them. Worse yet, he reportedly had a habit of poisoning his enemies.

With Alexander in view, we might actually find ourselves somewhat relieved that things in our day are no worse than they are. Pope John Paul II is a heroically holy man. We have not yet sunk to the point of languishing under a Successor of Peter whose life story reads like a sleazy Andrew Greeley novel.

Suffering and Hope

At this point we must be clear: In no way does the frequency through-out Church history of sexual sin among clergy and religious somehow lessen the seriousness of that sin or its consequences. Whether in the fourteenth century or the twenty-first, human nature is perverted, dis-ordered, corroded by sexual misconduct, with both abuser and victim profoundly injured. And the consequences are infinitely more grave—as St. Catherine, St. Bernard, and others have insisted—when the sin-ner is someone who carries the dignity and the responsibility of an *alter Christus.*

We must never even seem to suggest that the suffering of one of our contemporaries who is a victim of the current horror is no more than the dot of an "i" in the massive, depressing tome that is human history. Not at all. History, after all, has an end. The creature made in the image of God does not.

Long after the heavens and the earth have dissolved into ashes on God's hearth and blown away, immortal souls and their resurrected bodies will remain. They will forever carry the scars of their earthly suf-fering, for better or for worse. And it is the mission of the Church, Heaven help us, to see that those scars are transformed, like the nail holes in Christ's own flesh, into eternal testimonies to the Father's redemptive grace.

That is precisely why we must keep in mind the historical picture. If we conclude, through ignorance, that the Church has never faced such a trial as she faces today, we may despair. How can she possibly survive? How can we dare to hold on to her when she seems to be sink-ing into a deadly pit of chaos and oblivion?

Those in the media who ought to know more history than they do sometimes try to play on these fears. "Can the Catholic Church Be Saved?" shouted the garish headlines of a recent *Time* magazine cover story on the scandals. "If all this continues," says one supposed "leading Catholic" interviewed by the reporter, "the Church will disappear."

That "leading Catholic" should be told about a witty remark of Cardinal Ercole Casalvi, the brilliant nineteenth-century statesman to whom fell the difficult lot of negotiating with Napoleon as secretary of state for Pope Pius VII. Reports of his exact words vary, but the story runs something like this: One day the little tyrant flew into a rage over the Pope's refusal to meet his demands. The arrogant Frenchman screamed at the cardinal, "I will destroy your Church!"

"Your Majesty," Consalvi answered calmly, "if popes, cardinals, bishops, and priests have not succeeded in destroying the Church, how do you expect to do so?"

Dark humor, perhaps, yet the insight gives birth to hope. When we stop focusing so intently on today's sensational headlines and survey instead the two-thousand-year history of the Church, what do we see? An institution—no, an organism—so utterly tenacious, so resilient, so capable of renewal and, yes, even resurrection that we must confess in awe: "Her continued existence is an astounding miracle. The life within her must be supernatural!"

If the life within her is supernatural—and it is, because it is the life of Jesus Christ himself—then she will most certainly survive. More than that, she will be healed and renewed. If all the demon hosts cannot destroy her, then surely a handful of perverted priests, or even a horde of them, cannot do it. History abundantly illustrates the truth of Christ's own promise: "I will build my Church, and the gates of hell will not prevail against it" (see Mt 16:18).

For the victims and survivors of clerical abuse especially, the Church is thus the great model of hope. After all, she herself is a victim and survivor of abuse, some of it at the hands of her enemies, some at the hands of her children. Like her Master, she knows what it means to be betrayed, to be wounded, to be despised. And like her Master, she knows that beyond the grave lies glory.

Though she may lie on her deathbed a thousand times, she cannot remain there forever. The resurrected Son of God is her Life and her Lord. She will rise again.

A Diagnosis and Remedy

The restoration of the Church, though sure to come, does not come easily or quickly. Christ is the Great Physician, but the Church must take her medicine if she is to recover.

For an accurate diagnosis and effective treatment, we could do no better than to return to St. Catherine. This wise Doctor of the Church—"doctor" in more ways than one—listened carefully to her Lord as he examined the patient, spelled out the malady, and wrote his prescriptions. Then she recorded what she had heard in the *Dialogue*, reported it to the Church, and set out to administer the remedy.

Her entire book—or, at the very least, the section entitled "The Mystical Body of Holy Church"—should be required reading for every Catholic concerned about the current scandals (which is to say, I hope, every one of us). In the meantime, perhaps a brief overview of some of her insights will serve to point the way to new health in the Church.[1]

The Diagnosis

According to St. Catherine, the Lord spoke to her about several deeply rooted problems among the clergy, among them pride, a loss of sacred identity, a loss of faith, a tendency to worldliness, and pervasive sensuality. If we examine the Church today in light of each of these concerns, the parallels are clear. No doubt we can find many contemporary American bishops and priests who do not fit the profile she provides. But her words could nonetheless benefit all the clergy, religious, and laity if we use them as the basis for some honest self-examination.

Pride. "Pride," the Lord said to St. Catherine, "is both the end and the beginning" of all the other clerical vices. "All the vices are seasoned with pride, just as the virtues are seasoned and made alive by love."

In whatever class of people it may be found, the Lord insisted, pride displeases him. "But it displeases me much more in these ministers because I have appointed them to a humble state, to be servants of the humble Lamb. Yet they behave in just the opposite way."

Pride, St. Catherine noted, drives the bishops to ignore the plight of the little people. Instead, they focus on gaining the respect and support of the high and mighty in the world.

A loss of sacred identity. When we gaze on the infinitely precious sacrament of Christ's Body and Blood, says St. Catherine, we gaze into the abyss of God's love. No wonder, then, that when God speaks to her, he calls priests his "Christs." They have the incomparable dignity of ministering the fruits of Christ's passion to God's people—a dignity that not even the angels share.

Sadly, says St. Catherine, priests have forgotten or even denied their great dignity as Christ's own ministers. "They think they see," the Lord told her, "but they are actually blind: they do not know themselves, and they do not know me. They fail to know the status and the dignity to which I have appointed them."

From this loss of sacred identity, St. Catherine tells us, flow other problems. "Sins and abominations plague my Church," the Lord told her, because "those who appoint men to high offices do not investigate the lives of the men they appoint, to determine whether they are good or bad." Unworthy men are given high rank and great power because those who appoint them have so little sense of the gravity of the offices being filled.

A loss of faith. "The horns of your pride," God says to the priests through St. Catherine, "have stabbed the pupil of most holy faith in the eye of your mind. So you no longer have the light, and you cannot see how wretched you are. You do not believe that every sin has its punishment and every good its reward—if you did, you would not behave the way you do."

Lacking faith in God, they lose fear of God. The shepherds have lost their way; they have neither "the dog of conscience" to alert them to wrongdoing, nor the "rod of correction" to beat away the wolves from the flock. Yet ironically, having failed to fear God, they become spineless, "afraid of their own shadows—not with a holy fear, but with a slavish fear."

The loss of faith also shows itself in how the clergymen treat the Scripture. "These wretched ones ... neither perceive nor understand anything but the outer crust, the letter, of Scripture. They have no relish for it, because their spiritual sense of taste is disordered, corrupted, by selfish love and pride."

Yet another way in which loss of faith manifests itself among priests and bishops is in practices that are unorthodox and alien to the Christian tradition. They "cast spells and summon demons," St. Catherine complains. Instead of praying the Divine Office, they pray to devils. Instead of singing the traditional "psalms and hymns," they "resort to diabolical incantations."

Worldliness. An inordinate love of the world—and a fear of losing what it offers—can take many forms. St. Catherine identifies several types that plague the clergy of her day, making them "so miserably concerned about acquiring and holding on to temporal things that they seem to throw spiritual things behind them."

Most common, perhaps, is the "hankering for high ecclesiastical rank." When priests have worldly designs for their careers, they avoid making waves. "They pretend not to see" the sins around them that merit reproof; they refrain from correcting people "for fear of losing their rank and position." They are especially careful not to admonish powerful political leaders who are sinning openly.

She also reproves the clergy for extravagant lifestyles. Taking on the trappings of those around them who boast great status and wealth, the bishops live in fancy houses, wine and dine the "great men" of their day, waste the Church's money on unnecessarily expensive forms of travel, and spend too much time in frivolous pursuits.

Worldliness takes other forms as well. The priests love giving homilies of polished but empty rhetoric instead of proclaiming the word of God. They also have an inordinate desire for worldly education. This is not a chaste love for learning, St. Catherine notes, but a proud craving to be admired for erudition, and a disdain for those who are unlearned.

Sensuality. "If they had remembered their dignity as priests," the Lord says to St. Catherine, "they would not have stumbled into the darkness of mortal sin nor muddied the face of their souls." But instead they "feed and wallow in the mire of impurity."

"What is the source of such uncleanness in their souls? Their own selfish sensuality. Their selfishness has made a mistress of their sensuality, and their miserable little souls have become her slaves." Like worldliness, St. Catherine points out, sensuality takes a variety of forms among the clergy: inordinate eating and drinking, gutter language, materialism, and—worst of all—sexual impurity.

The pages of the *Dialogue* are seared with fiery condemnations of sexual sin. "O demons, and worse than demons!" the Lord says to fornicating priests. "They rise in the morning with their minds corrupted and their bodies defiled. After spending the night in bed with mortal sin, they go to celebrate Mass! O tabernacles of the devil!"

"I let them bind my Son's hands to set you and all humankind free from sin's bondage," the Lord reminds them. "I anointed and consecrated your hands for the ministry of the Most Holy Sacrament. Yet you use your hands for disgusting obscene touching!"

Worse yet is the abomination of homosexual impurity, that "cursed unnatural sin." The "stench" of this sin not only offends heaven, says the Lord; even the demons themselves loathe the odor of it and run away. In St. Catherine's day, "it seemed as if you could not live among the lowly or the mighty, religious or clergymen, superiors or subjects, masters or servants; for they were all stained in mind and body by this curse." But this particular sin is "much more hateful" to God in those who are called to celibacy.

Bishops who are guilty of sexual impurity lose their moral leverage and blind themselves to the reality of sin. "They will not correct the sins of others," says the Lord to St. Catherine, "because they themselves are living in the same or greater sins. They realize that the same guilt surrounds them, so they throw out their zeal and trust and, in the chains of slavish fear, pretend that they do not see.... How can men who are so sinful bring their subjects to righteousness and rebuke them for their sins? They cannot do so, for their own sins have stolen from them any enthusiasm or fervor for holy righteousness."

The result of all this wickedness, God tells her, is a fast track to damnation. He minces no words: "In hell ... these wicked ministers will be more severely punished than other Christians who committed the very same sins, because of the ministry I gave to them when I made them stewards of ... the Holy Sacrament, and because they had the light of learning by which they could have discerned the truth for themselves as well as for others—if they had only chosen to do so. So it is just that they should be most severely punished."

Is there a place for divine mercy here? Of course! "With my mercy," God promises, "they can gain access to hope—if only they are willing. Otherwise, not a one of them would fail to despair, and despair would bring everlasting damnation with the demons."

The Remedy

What can be done to restore health to the Church? St. Catherine offers these further insights from her conversations with God.

Rome must take decisive action to discipline offending bishops. The pope, whom St. Catherine refers to as "Christ on earth," has the duty of delegating ministers to help him in service to the Church. Only those he has "accepted and consecrated" can minister as bishops, and he is "the head of the whole clerical order."

The Lord said to her: "Because the pope has sent these men out as his assistants, it is his responsibility to correct them for their faults, and it is my will that he do just that." When he is aware of sin among the bishops, he should chastise them; "he should take out of office those who will not repent and turn from their wicked way of living."

If the pope does this, he is performing his sacred duty. If not, "his sin will not go unpunished when it is his turn to give an accounting for the little ones of his flock."

The bishops and other high Church officials must take decisive action against offending priests. In a vivid image, St. Catherine rebukes bishops who have failed to discipline their priests through a misguided notion of "mercy." Those who will not receive correction and those who will not give it, she says, are like limbs of a body beginning to rot.

"If a doctor only applied salve to a wound without cauterizing it first, the whole body would become stinking and rotten," she observes. "It is the same with prelates and others in authority. If they see among their subjects those who are rotting because of the putrefaction of deadly sin, and yet they only apply the salve of soft words without rebuke, they will never be healed. Instead, they will infect the other members of the Body."

And what of those who are "obstinate in their wickedness"? They must be "cut off from the congregation so that they will not infect the whole Body with the foulness of mortal sin."

Lay people must not allow themselves to be scandalized to the point of withdrawing from the sacraments. The sinfulness of the clergy can never "deprive the Blood of Christ in the Eucharist or any other sacrament of its perfection." So we must not turn away from the precious gift of the sacraments simply because of the wretchedness and unworthiness of those who bear the gift.

"If someone dirty or dressed in rags were to bring you a great life-giving treasure," the Lord said to St. Catherine, "you would not disdain the gift-bearer for love of the treasure itself and the lord who sent it to you." In a similar way, because we so desperately need the life-giving treasure of the sacraments, we should receive it at the hands even of sinful priests. "If you receive these sacraments worthily, and for love of me, the eternal God, who sends them to you, and for love of the life of grace that you receive from this great treasure, then you receive grace through them no matter how sinful the bearers might be."

Lay people must not use the situation as an excuse to denigrate priests in general. Some of St. Catherine's sharpest rebukes are directed to lay people who are "irreverent persecutors" of the clergy. In fact, she reports that Christ said to her, "To me accrues every assault they make on my ministers: derision, slander, disgrace, abuse."

Despite the legitimate anger and sense of betrayal many Catholics feel, the priesthood is still worthy of great respect: "For no sin in the priest," the Lord said to St. Catherine, "can lessen the power of the Sacrament, and thus their reverence for the priest who administers the Sacrament should not lessen either."

The entire Church must earnestly pray. All the faithful, God said, have a special role in such a crisis: "I set among the wicked my servants who are healthy and not diseased in order to pray for them."

"Now, my most dear daughter," the Lord told St. Catherine, "I invite you and all my other servants to weep over these priests who are spiritually dead. Be like little lambs in the garden of Holy Church, grazing there in a holy longing and continual prayer. Offer your desires and your prayers to me for their sakes so that I can show mercy to the world.... Be humble and attentive to my honor, the salvation of souls, and the reform of Holy Church. This will be a sign to me that you truly love me."

God told St. Catherine he would answer such ardent, persistent prayers. Just as the Church is now filled with troubles, it will abound with joy and consolation. The "good holy shepherds" will become like "flowers of glory," blossoming with "the fragrance of virtue rooted in truth."

With St. Catherine, then—who no doubt is praying fervently for the Church even now—we must take hope and give ourselves to intercession for all victims and survivors, bishops and priests, lay and religious, abusers, and all those who have been affected by the scandals of our day. God promises us, as he promised her, that even though the healing will be costly, it will be sure: "For I, Eternal Truth, promise to refresh you. And after your bitterness I will grant you consolation—with great suffering—in the reform of Holy Church."

Paul Thigpen is a senior editor for Servant Publications. He holds a Ph.D. in historical theology from Emory University in Atlanta and is the author or compiler of twenty-six books, including Blood of the Martyrs, Seed of the Church *and* The Rapture Trap: A Catholic Response to "End Times" Fever.

[1] In my extensive quotes of St. Catherine in this essay—all from the *Dialogue*—I am using translations or paraphrases of my own. For a fine English translation of this spiritual classic, see *Catherine of Siena: The Dialogue*, translated by Suzanne Noffke (New York: Paulist Press, 1980).

We should note here that St. Catherine's claims to have heard God speak to her about these matters are a matter of private revelation rather than public revelation, so Catholics are not obliged by the Church to accept them as authentic. yet even for those who conclude that the *Dialogue* simply represents her own thought in the light of Scripture, Tradition, and personal experience, the text should carry considerable weight: She is, after all, a Doctor of the Church, and these words come from a woman of extraordinary intellect, holiness, and spiritual gifts whose wisdom has proven fruitful in the lives of Christians for centuries.

III: Scripture Readings, Reflections, and Prayers

"Have Mercy Upon Us, O Lord"

Scripture Readings

✦ Judgment ✦

For the time has come for judgment to begin with the household of God.

1 PETER 4:17

Nothing is covered up that will not be revealed, or hidden that will not be known. Whatever you have said in the dark shall be heard in the light, and what you have whispered in private rooms shall be proclaimed from the housetops.

LUKE 12:2-3

Do not be deceived; God is not mocked, for whatever a man sows, that he will also reap. For he who sows to his own flesh will from the flesh reap corruption; but he who sows to the Spirit will from the Spirit reap eternal life.

GALATIANS 6:7-8

Whoever receives one such child in my name receives me; but whoever causes one of these little ones who believe in me to sin, it would be better for him to have a great millstone fastened round his neck and to be drowned in the depth of the sea.

MATTHEW 18:5-6

You shall not lie with a male as with a woman; it is an abomination.

LEVITICUS 18:22

For the wrath of God is revealed from heaven against all ungodliness and wickedness of men who by their wickedness suppress the truth. … Therefore God gave them up in the lusts of their hearts to impurity, to the dishonoring of their bodies among themselves, because they exchanged the truth about God for a lie and worshipped and served the creature rather than the Creator, who is blessed forever! Amen.

For this reason God gave them up to dishonorable passions. Their women exchanged natural relations for unnatural, and the men likewise gave up natural relations with women and were consumed with passion for one another, men committing shameless acts with men and receiving in their own persons the due penalty for their error.

ROMAN 18, 24-27

The word of the Lord came to me: … "[Israel's] priests have done violence to my law and have profaned my holy things; they have made no distinction between the holy and the common, neither have they taught the difference between the unclean and the clean, and they have disregarded my sabbaths, so that I am profaned among them…. Her prophets have daubed for them with whitewash, seeing false visions and divining lies for them, saying, 'Thus says the Lord God,' when the Lord has not spoken…. Therefore I have poured out my indignation upon them; I have consumed them with the fire of my wrath; their way have I requited upon their heads, says the Lord God."

EZEKIEL 22:23, 26, 28, 31

But false prophets also arose among the people, just as there will be false teachers among you, who will secretly bring in destructive heresies, even denying the Master who bought them, bringing upon themselves swift destruction. And many will follow their licentiousness, and because of them the way of truth will be reviled. And in their greed they will exploit you with false words; from of old their condemnation has not been idle, and their destruction has not been asleep....

These are waterless springs and mists driven by a storm; for them the nether gloom of darkness has been reserved. For, uttering loud boasts of folly, they entice with licentious passions of the flesh men who have barely escaped from those who live in error. They promise them freedom, but they themselves are slaves of corruption; for whatever overcomes a man, to that he is enslaved.

2 PETER 2:1-3, 17-19

It is actually reported that there is immorality among you.... And you are arrogant [about it]! Ought you not rather to mourn? Let him who has done this be removed from among you.... You are to deliver this man to Satan for the destruction of the flesh, that his spirit may be saved in the day of the Lord Jesus.

1 CORINTHIANS 5:1-2, 5

The two sons of Eli [the priest] ... were priests of the Lord.... Now the sons of Eli were worthless men; they had no regard for the Lord.... The sin of the young men was very great in the sight of the Lord; for the men treated the offering of the Lord with contempt....

Now Eli was very old, and he heard all that his sons were doing to all Israel, and how they lay with the women who served at the entrance to the tent of meeting. And he said to them, "Why do you do such things? For I hear of your evil dealings from all the people. No, my sons; it is no good report that I hear the people of the Lord spreading abroad. If a man sins against a man, God will mediate for him; but if a man sins against the Lord, who can intercede for him?"

But they would not listen to the voice of their father; for it was the will of the Lord to slay them. ...

And there came a man of God to Eli, and said to him, "Thus the Lord has said ... 'Those who honor me I will honor, and those who despise me shall be lightly esteemed. Behold, the days are coming, when I will cut off your strength and the strength of your father's house, so that there will not be an old man in your house....

Then the Lord said to Samuel [who was serving Eli the priest] ... "Tell him that I am about to punish his house for ever, for the iniquity which he knew [about], because his sons were blaspheming God, and he did not restrain them."

1 SAMUEL 1:3; 2:12, 17, 22-25; 27, 30-31; 3:11, 13

✦ Repentance ✦

Bear fruit that befits repentance.

MATTHEW 3:8

Therefore, having this ministry by the mercy of God, we do not lose heart. We have renounced disgraceful, underhanded ways; we refuse to practice cunning or to tamper with God's word, but by the open statement of the truth we would commend ourselves to every man's conscience in the sight of God.

2 CORINTHIANS 4:1-2

For a bishop, as God's steward, must be blameless; he must not be arrogant or quick-tempered or a drunkard or violent or greedy for gain, but hospitable, a lover of goodness, master of himself, upright, holy, and self-controlled; he must hold firm to the sure word as taught, so that he may be able to give instruction in sound doctrine and also to confute those who contradict it.

TITUS 1:7-9

If we say we have no sin, we deceive ourselves, and the truth is not in us. If we confess our sins, he is faithful and just, and will forgive our sins and cleanse us from all unrighteousness. If we say we have not sinned, we make him a liar, and his word is not in us.

1 JOHN 1:8-10

Blessed is he whose transgression is forgiven,
　　whose sin is covered.
　　　　Blessed is the man to whom the Lord imputes no iniquity,
　　　　　　and in whose spirit there is no deceit.
When I declared not my sin, my body wasted away
　　through my groaning all day long.
　　　　For day and night thy hand was heavy upon me;
　　　　　　my strength was dried up as by the heat of summer.
I acknowledged my sin to thee,
　　and I did not hide my iniquity;
　　　　I said, "I will confess my transgressions to the Lord,"
　　　　　　then thou didst forgive the guilt of my sin.

PSALM 32:1-5

✦ Mercy ✦

Where sin increased, grace abounded all the more.

ROMANS 5:20

Be mindful of thy mercy, O Lord, and of thy steadfast love,
    for they have been from of old.
Remember not the sins of my youth, or my transgressions;
    according to thy steadfast love remember me,
    for thy goodness' sake, O Lord!
Good and upright is the Lord;
    therefore he instructs sinners in the way.

PSALM 25:6-8

Behold, as the eyes of servants look to the hand of their master, as the eyes of a maid to the hand of her mistress, so our eyes look to the Lord our God, till he have mercy upon us. Have mercy upon us, O Lord, have mercy upon us, for we have had more than enough of contempt.

PSALM 123:2-3

And you he made alive, when you were dead through the trespasses and sins in which you once walked, following the course of this world, following the prince of the power of the air, the spirit that is now at work in the sons of disobedience. Among these we all once lived in the passions of our flesh, following the desires of body and mind, and so we were by nature children of wrath, like the rest of mankind. But God, who is rich in mercy, out of the great love with which he loved us, even when we were dead through our trespasses, made us alive together with Christ (by grace you have been saved), and raised us up with him, and made us sit with him in the heavenly places in Christ Jesus, that in the coming ages he might show the immeasurable riches of his grace in kindness toward us in Christ Jesus.

EPHESIANS 2:1-7

✦ Forgiveness and Restoration ✦

Father, forgive them; for they know not what they do.

LUKE 23:34

Let all bitterness and wrath and anger and clamor and slander be put away from you, with all malice, and be kind to one another, tenderhearted, forgiving one another, as God in Christ forgave you.

EPHESIANS 4:31-32

Brethren, if a man is overtaken in any trespass, you who are spiritual should restore him in a spirit of gentleness. Look to yourself, lest you too be tempted. Bear one another's burdens, and so fulfil the law of Christ.

GALATIANS 6:1-2

Put on then, as God's chosen ones, holy and beloved, compassion, kindness, lowliness, meekness, and patience, forbearing one another and, if one has a complaint against another, forgiving each other; as the Lord has forgiven you, so you also must forgive. And above all these put on love, which binds everything together in perfect harmony. And let the peace of Christ rule in your hearts, to which indeed you were called in one body.

COLOSSIANS 3:12-15

✦ Hope ✦

You will know the truth, and the truth will make you free.

JOHN 8:32

Why are you cast down, O my soul,
   and why are you disquieted within me?
Hope in God; for I shall again praise him,
   my help and my God.

PSALM 42:5

I waited patiently for the Lord;
   he inclined to me and heard my cry.
He drew me up from the desolate pit,
   out of the miry bog,
   and set my feet upon a rock,
   making my steps secure.
He put a new song in my mouth,
   a song of praise to our God.
Many will see and fear,
   and put their trust in the Lord.
Blessed is the man who makes the Lord his trust.

PSALM 40:1-4

For the Lord has chosen Zion;
   he has desired it for his habitation:
"This is my resting place forever;
   here I will dwell, for I have desired it.
I will abundantly bless her provisions;

I will satisfy her poor with bread.
Her priests I will clothe with salvation,
    and her saints will shout for joy."

PSALM 132:13-17

Do you not know that the unrighteous will not inherit the kingdom of God? Do not be deceived: neither the immoral, nor idolaters, nor adulterers, nor [practicing] homosexuals, nor thieves, nor the greedy, nor drunkards, nor revilers, nor robbers will inherit the kingdom of God. And such were some of you. But you were washed, you were sanctified, you were justified in the name of the Lord Jesus Christ and in the Spirit of our God.

1 CORINTHIANS 6:9-11

We know that in everything God works for good with those who love him, who are called according to his purpose.

ROMANS 8:28

For I am sure that neither death, nor life, nor angels, nor principalities, nor things present, nor things to come, nor powers, nor height, nor depth, nor anything else in all creation, will be able to separate us from the love of God in Christ Jesus our Lord.

ROMANS 8:38

On this rock I will build my church, and the powers of death will not prevail against it.

MATTHEW 16:18

"Truth Suffers, but Never Dies"

Reflections

✦ On the Nature of the Church ✦

How much I must criticize you, my Church, and yet how much I love you. You have made me suffer more than anyone, and yet I owe more to you than anyone. I should like to see you destroyed, and yet I need your presence. You have given me much scandal and yet you alone have made me understand holiness. Never in this world have I seen anything more compromised, more false, yet never have I touched anything more pure, more generous, and more beautiful.

Countless times I have felt like slamming the door of my soul in your face, and yet, every night, I have prayed that I might die in your sure arms. No. I cannot be free of you, for I am one with you, even if not completely you.

Then too ... where would I go? To build another church? But I could not build one without the same defects, for they are my defects, and again, if I were to build another church, it would be my church, not Christ's church. No, I am old enough. I know better.

Carlo Carretto, *I Sought and I Found*

All your dissatisfaction with the Church seems to me to come from an incomplete understanding of sin.... What you seem actually to demand is that the Church put the kingdom of heaven on earth right here now, that the Holy Ghost be translated at once into all flesh.... You are asking that man return at once to the state God created him in, you are leaving out the terrible radical human pride that causes death. Christ was crucified on earth and the Church is crucified in time, and the Church is crucified by all of us, by her members most particularly because she is a Church of sinners. Christ never said that the Church would be operated in a sinless or intelligent way, but that it would not teach error.... The Church is founded on Peter who denied Christ three times and couldn't walk on the water by himself. You are expecting his successors to walk on the water. All human nature vigorously resists grace because grace changes us and the change is painful. Priests resist it as well as others. To have the Church be what you want it to be would require the continuous miraculous meddling of God in human affairs, whereas it is our dignity that we are allowed more or less to get on with those graces that come through faith and the sacraments and which work through our human nature.

Flannery O'Connor, *The Habit of Being*

It was ever in my mind that human frailties and the sins and ignorances of those in high places throughout history only proved that the Church *must* be divine to have persisted through the centuries. I would not blame the Church for what I felt were the mistakes of churchmen.

Dorothy Day, *The Long Loneliness*

At the end of time, death, the last enemy, will be destroyed, and the one and only house of Rahab, the one and only Church, will be delivered from the destruction of the ungodly, at last pure and free of the shame of fornication through the window of confession in the blood of the remission of sins. Until this happens, as long as the world lasts, the Church remains as a harlot in Jericho.

St. Isidore of Seville, *On Old and New Testament Questions*

To be "a glorious Church not having spot or wrinkle" [see Eph 5:27] is the ultimate end to which we are brought by the passion of Christ. Hence this will be in heaven and not on earth, where, "if we say we have no sin, we deceive ourselves," as it is written [1 Jn 1:8].

St. Thomas Aquinas, *Summa Theologica*

Christianity has had a series of revolutions and in each one of them Christianity has died. Christianity has died many times and risen again; for it had a God who knew the way out of the grave....

It would seem that sooner or later even [the Church's] enemies will learn from their incessant and interminable disappointments not to look for anything so simple as its death. They may continue to war with it, but it will be as they war with nature; as they war with the landscape, as they war with the skies. "Heaven and earth shall pass way, but my words shall not pass away" [see Mt 24:35]. They will watch for it to stumble; they will watch for it to err; they will no longer watch for it to end. Insensibly, even unconsciously, they will in their own silent anticipations fulfill the relative terms of that astounding prophecy; they will forget to watch for the mere extinction of what has so often been vainly extinguished; and will learn instinctively to look first for the coming of the comet or the freezing of the star.

G. K. Chesterton, *The Everlasting Man*

✦ On Church Scandals and Crisis ✦

Truly, matters in the world are in a bad state; but if you and I begin in earnest to reform ourselves, a really good beginning will have been made.

St. Peter of Alcantara

Since the Church began aiming more at temporal things than at spiritual, things have gone from bad to worse.

St. Catherine of Siena to Pope Gregory XI

"These are bad times," people are saying, "troublesome times!" If only our lives were all good, our times would be good, for we ourselves make our times—as we are, so are our times. But what can we do? After all, we cannot convert the mass of humanity to a good life. But let the few who do listen to the will of God live good lives; and let the few who live good lives endure the many who do not. The good are the wheat, still on the threshing floor; and though the chaff lies with them there, the chaff will not come with them to the barn.

St. Augustine of Hippo

The past must be abandoned to God's mercy, the present to our faithfulness, the future to divine providence.

St. Francis de Sales

Giving scandal may lead to spiritual murder. Taking scandal may lead to spiritual suicide.

Adapted from St. Francis de Sales

For certainly no one does more harm in the Church than the one who bears the name and office of holiness while acting wickedly. For no one dares to take him to task when he transgresses, and so the sin spreads forcibly by his example, because the sinner is honored out of reverence for his office.

Pope St. Gregory the Great, *On Pastoral Rule*

Those who wage war against the truth are powerless to win; rather, they wound themselves, like those who kick against spikes.

St. John Chrysostom

Error may flourish for a time, but truth will prevail in the end. The only effect of error ultimately is to promote truth.

Venerable Cardinal John Henry Newman

Truth suffers, but never dies.

St. Teresa of Avila

Divine assistance for the Church is not restricted to the first centuries of the Church, but is continued and will be continued to the end of time. This reflection has calmed my spirit on more than one occasion. May it serve to calm yours when you witness error worming about.

Blessed Dominic Barbieri

This is, at bottom, a crisis of fidelity. It will not be resolved by the Church adopting a "Catholic Lite" strategy—abandoning priestly celibacy, dumbing down Catholic sexual ethics—as progressive joy riders on the crisis are suggesting.

Catholic Lite helped cause the crisis. The path to genuine reform is for the Church to become more Catholic, not less.

George Weigel

✦ On the Clergy ✦

A monk who lived alone in the desert was scandalized when someone made accusations against the character of the priest who came regularly to bring him Holy Communion. The next time the priest came, the monk turned him away.

Then the monk heard a voice saying: "Men have taken my judgment into their own hands." And he was caught up in a trance, and saw a vision of a golden well with a golden bucket on a golden rope, filled with good drinking water. There was a leper filling and emptying and refilling the bucket.

The monk was quite thirsty for the water, but he refused to drink any because the bucket had been filled by the leper. Then the voice came a second time to him, saying, "Why don't you drink the water? What does it matter who fills the bucket? He only fills it, pours it out, and fills it again."

Finally the monk came back to his senses and understood what the vision had meant. So he called the priest to bring him Holy Communion as before.

The Sayings of the Desert Fathers

There is an element in the life and witness of priests on which I must put special emphasis. It is the radical gift of priestly celibacy. The discussions which have taken place too often cloud the meaning of this commitment and cause a lack of understanding in regard to those who live it generously. Could we not make our contemporaries understand better that this is a free gift of self, a self-mastery which not only allows for greater availability, but above all is a total belonging to him for whom one has offered one's life, who offered himself for all people?

This renunciation, lived in humble fidelity, is a freely chosen way of dedicating one's life which does not detract from one's personality. In a communion of deep love for good and true openness to others, celibacy for the sake of the kingdom allows for real personal growth and provides an authentic witness of generosity. Every day we discover this in the priests around us because they reveal with simplicity that men can take their emotional life and offer it to God.

Pope John Paul II, *"Spirituality for Diocesan Priests"*

In regard to what constitutes priestly life ... I would say that the messengers of the gospel must be evangelized themselves. They must understand the need for allowing themselves to be taken hold of by Christ, in the fervor of the Spirit. They experience the need of opening their hearts and minds as men of today to God's self-revelation in Christ, so as to be his true witnesses. Thus, the spiritual quest cannot be separated from the effort to understand the faith, for our contemporaries expect us to lead them towards the light.

Pope John Paul II, *"Spirituality for Diocesan Priests"*

The bishop should be, through humility, a companion of those who live morally good lives, and, through the zeal of righteousness, rigid against the vices of evildoers. In this way, then, he will never show preference to his own interests while he is with those who are good, and yet, when the fault of those who are bad requires it, he will at once be conscious of his authority. The result will be that while among his priests who live righteously, he will lay aside his rank and count them as equals. But toward those who are perverse he will have no fear in executing the laws of righteousness....

For the bishop is rightly numbered among the hypocrites if under the pretense of discipline he turns the ministry of governing the Church into domination. And yet sometimes there is a more grievous delinquency, if among perverse priests he acts as an equal rather than exercising discipline.

Pope St. Gregory the Great, *The Pastoral Rule*

"Source of All Consolation and Hope"

Prayers

✦ For the Victims, Survivors, and Children ✦

Praise to you, Father of our Lord Jesus Christ,
    source of all consolation and hope.
By your Son's dying and rising
    He remains our light in every darkness,
        our strength in every weakness.
Be the refuge and guardian
    of all who suffer from abuse and violence.
Comfort them and send healing
    for their wounds of body, soul, and spirit.
Rescue them from bitterness and shame
    and refresh them with your love.
Heal the brokenness in all victims of abuse
    and revive the spirits of all who lament this sin.
Help us to follow Jesus
    in drawing good from evil, life from death.
Make us one with you in your love for justice
    as we deepen our respect
        for the dignity of every human life.
Giver of peace,
    make us one in celebrating your praise,
        both now and for ever. *Amen.*

Office for Divine Worship, Archdiocese of Chicago

O Lord, be the Shepherd of these victims and survivors
    so they may lack nothing for their healing.
Show them green pastures where they can lie down at last to rest.
    Lead them gently to the place where they can drink
        from the still waters of peace they have sought for so long.
Restore their souls to wholeness.
Lead them in the paths of righteousness,
    show them the way to justice, so that those who bear your Name
        will cease to be a stumbling block to them.
Yes, when they walk through the valley of the shadows
    of death, of despair, of depression,
        of questions without answers, of terrors unnamed,
            be with them.
With your mighty rod and staff comfort and protect them.
Drive away forever the preying memories that feed on their souls.
Prepare for them a feast of forgiveness in the presence of their enemies
    where their daily bread will no longer be bitter.
Anoint their heads with the oil of laughter they once knew as children
    before their innocence was stolen.
Fill their cups to overflowing with new life and song.
    Let your goodness and mercy be their faithful companions
        all the days of their lives
            and bring them safely home
                to live in the light of your face forever. *Amen.*

Adapted from Psalm 23 by Paul Thigpen

May the Blessed Virgin, who had the joy of bringing and holding in her arms the Son of God made a Child, of seeing him grow in wisdom, age, and grace before God and man, help each one of us to endow his personal efforts on behalf of little children with active goodness, an attractive example, and self-giving love. *Amen.*

Pope John Paul II

✦ For the Clergy ✦

Arise, O Lord.... Let thy priests be clothed with righteousness, and let thy saints shout for joy.

PSALM 132:8-9

We entreat thee, Almighty Father, to give these servants of thine the dignity of priesthood. Renew in them the Spirit of holiness, so that by holding, by thy gift, the second rank in thy service, they may so conduct their daily lives as to set an example of holy living. May they be prudent helpers in the work of our Order, and radiant with every virtue, so that they may be able to give a good account of the stewardship committed to them and to gain the reward of eternal happiness. Through the same Jesus Christ, thy Son, our Lord, who is God, living and reigning with thee, in the unity of the same Holy Spirit, forever and ever. Amen.

From a Rite of Ordination of Priests

May your every word and deed be an eloquent witness to our God
   who is rich in mercy.
May your sermons inspire hope in the mercy of the Redeemer.
May the way you celebrate the sacrament of Penance help each person
   experience in a unique way the merciful love of God, which is more
      powerful than sin.
And may your own personal kindness and pastoral love help everyone
   you meet to discover the merciful Father, who is always ready to forgive.
Amen.

Pope John Paul II

God, who alone can sanctify, to whom alone belongs true consecration
and fullness of benediction, pour forth the gift of thy blessing upon
these servants of thine, whom we are dedicating to the office of priesthood. May they show themselves, by their grave conduct, and by the
whole pattern of their lives, to be true elders, grounded in the teaching which Paul gave to Timothy and Titus.

Let them ponder thy law day and night, believe what they read,
preach what they believe, and practice what they preach.

May they be living models, prompting others by word and example to follow them in justice and steadfastness, in compassion and for-
titude, and in all other virtues.

May they keep the gift of thy ministry pure and undefiled. Let their
blessing be untainted when they transform bread and wine thereby, for
the service of thy people, into the Body and Blood of thy Son.

And at the day of God's just and irrevocable judgment may they rise
again, filled with the Holy Spirit, in pure conscience, loyal faith, and
flawless love, to reach perfect manhood, proportioned to the completed
growth of Christ; through the same Jesus Christ, thy Son, our Lord,

who is God, living and reigning with thee in the unity of the same Holy Spirit, for ever and ever. *Amen.*

From a Rite of Ordination of Priests

O Mary, Mother of Jesus Christ and Mother of Priests, accept this title which we bestow on you to celebrate your motherhood and to contemplate with you the priesthood of your Son and of your sons, O Holy Mother of God.

O Mother of Christ, to the Messiah-Priest you gave a body of flesh through the anointing of the Holy Spirit for the salvation of the poor and the contrite of heart; guard priests in your heart and in the Church, O Mother of the Savior.

O Mother of Faith, you accompanied to the temple the Son of Man, the fulfillment of the promises given to the fathers; give to the Father for his glory the priests of your Son, O Ark of the Covenant.

O Mother of the Church, in the midst of the disciples in the Upper Room you prayed to the Spirit for the new people and their shepherds; obtain for the Order of Presbyters a full measure of gifts, O Queen of the Apostles.

O Mother of Jesus Christ, you were with him at the beginning of his life and mission, you sought the Master among the crowd, you stood beside him when he was lifted up from the earth consumed as the one eternal sacrifice, and you had John, your son, near at hand; accept from the beginning those who have been called, protect their growth, in their life ministry accompany your sons, O Mother of Priests. *Amen.*

Pope John Paul II, *"I Will Give You Shepherds"*

O God, who to glorify your sovereign power and for the salvation of humankind ordained your only-begotten Son a High Priest forever, grant that those whom he has chosen to be his ministers and the stewards of his mysteries may be found faithful in fulfilling the office committed to them, through the same Christ our Lord. *Amen.*

☀ Litany of Our Lord Jesus Christ, Priest and Victim ☀

According to Pope John Paul II, this litany has been customarily recited at the seminary in Cracow, Poland, especially on the day before ordinations. This English version is not an official translation.

Lord, have mercy. ....*Lord, have mercy.*

Christ, have mercy. ....*Christ, have mercy.*

Lord, have mercy. ....*Lord, have mercy.*

Christ, heed our prayer. ....*Christ, heed our prayer.*

Father in heaven, God, ...*Have mercy on us.*

Son, Redeemer of the world, God, ...*Have mercy on us.*

Holy Spirit, God, ...*Have mercy on us.*

Holy Trinity, one God, ...*Have mercy on us.*

Jesus, Priest and Victim, ...*Have mercy on us.*

Jesus, Priest forever,
   according to the order of Melchizedek, ...*Have mercy on us.*

Jesus, Priest sent by God
   to preach the Gospel to the poor, ...*Have mercy on us.*

Jesus, Priest who at the Last Supper
   instituted the form of the Eternal Sacrifice, ...*Have mercy on us.*

Jesus, Priest living forever
  to make intercession for us,...*Have mercy on us.*
Jesus, High Priest whom the Father
  anointed with the Holy Spirit and virtue, ...*Have mercy on us.*
Jesus, High Priest
  taken up from among men, ...*Have mercy on us.*
Jesus, made High Priest for men,...............................*Have mercy on us.*
Jesus, High Priest
  of our Confession of Faith, ...*Have mercy on us.*
Jesus, High Priest
  of greater glory than Moses,............................ ....*Have mercy on us.*
Jesus, High Priest of the true Tabernacle, ...*Have mercy on us.*
Jesus, High Priest of good things to come,..................*Have mercy on us.*
Jesus, holy High Priest,
  innocent and undefiled, ...*Have mercy on us.*
Jesus, faithful and merciful High Priest, ...*Have mercy on us.*
Jesus, High Priest of God,
  on fire with zeal for souls, ...*Have mercy on us.*
Jesus, perfect High Priest forever, ...*Have mercy on us.*
Jesus, High Priest
  who pierced Heaven with Your own Blood, ...*Have mercy on us.*
Jesus, High Priest
  who initiated us into a new life,................................*Have mercy on us.*
Jesus, High Priest who loved us and washed
  us clean of our sins in your Blood, ...*Have mercy on us.*
Jesus, High Priest, who gave yourself up
  to God as offering and victim, ...*Have mercy on us.*
Jesus, sacrificial Victim of God and man, ...*Have mercy on us.*
Jesus, holy and spotless sacrificial Victim, ...*Have mercy on us.*

Jesus, mild and gentle sacrificial Victim, ...*Have mercy on us.*

Jesus, peace-making sacrificial Victim, ...*Have mercy on us.*

Jesus, sacrificial Victim
of propitiation and praise, ...*Have mercy on us.*

Jesus, sacrificial Victim
of reconciliation and peace, ...*Have mercy on us.*

Jesus, sacrificial Victim in whom
we have confidence and access to God,....................*Have mercy on us.*

Jesus, sacrificial Victim living
forever and ever, ...*Have mercy on us.*

Be gracious! ....*Spare us, Jesus.*

Be gracious! ....*Hear us, Jesus.*

From rashly entering the clergy, ...*Free us, Jesus.*

From the sin of sacrilege, ...*Free us, Jesus.*

From the spirit of incontinence, ...*Free us, Jesus.*

From sordid self-interest,..*Free us, Jesus.*

From every lapse into simony,..*Free us, Jesus.*

From the unworthy administration
of the Church's treasures, ...*Free us, Jesus.*

From the love of the world and its vanities,......................*Free us, Jesus.*

From the unworthy celebration
of your Mysteries, ...*Free us, Jesus.*

Through your eternal priesthood,.....................................*Free us, Jesus.*

Through the holy anointing by which
God the Father made you a priest, ...*Free us, Jesus.*

Through your priestly spirit, ...*Free us, Jesus.*

Through the ministry by which you
  glorified your Father on this earth, ...*Free us, Jesus.*
Through the bloody immolation of yourself
  made once and for all on the cross, ...*Free us, Jesus.*
Through that same sacrifice
  daily renewed on the altar, ...*Free us, Jesus.*
Through the divine power that you
  exercise invisibly in your priests, ...*Free us, Jesus.*

That you may kindly maintain the whole priestly order in holy religion,
  Hear us, we beseech you.
That you may kindly provide your people with pastors after your
  own heart,
  Hear us, we beseech you.
That you may kindly fill them with the spirit of your priesthood,
  Hear us, we beseech you.
That the lips of your priests may be repositories of knowledge,
  Hear us, we beseech you.
That you may kindly send faithful workers into your harvest,
  Hear us, we beseech you.
That you may kindly increase the faithful dispensers of your mysteries,
  Hear us, we beseech you.
That you may kindly grant them persevering obedience to your will,
  Hear us, we beseech you.
That you may kindly give them gentleness in their ministry, skill in
  their actions, and constancy in their prayer,
  Hear us, we beseech you.
That through them, you may kindly promote the veneration of the
  Blessed Sacrament all over the world,

Hear us, we beseech you.

That you may kindly receive into your joy those who have served you well,

Hear us, we beseech you.

Lamb of God, who takes away the sins of the world,

Spare us, O Lord.

Lamb of God, who takes away the sins of the world,

Graciously hear us, O Lord.

Lamb of God, who takes away the sins of the world,

Have mercy on us, O Lord.

Jesus, our Priest, ...*Hear us.*

Jesus, our Priest, ...*Heed our prayers.*

Let us pray.

O God, sanctifier and guardian of your Church, stir up in her, through your Spirit, suitable and faithful dispensers of the Holy Mysteries, so that by their ministry and example, the Christian people may be guided in the path of salvation with your protection. Through Christ, our Lord. *Amen.*

God, who, when the disciples ministered to the Lord and fasted, ordered that Saul and Barnabas be set aside for the work to which you called them, be with your Church as she prays now, and may you, who know the hearts of all of us, show those whom you have chosen for your ministry. Through Christ, Our Lord. *Amen.*

✦ For the Abusers ✦

Out of the depths I cry to thee, O Lord!
Lord, hear my voice!
Let thy ears be attentive to the voice of my supplications!
If thou, O Lord, shouldst mark iniquities,
Lord, who could stand?
But there is forgiveness with thee,
that thou mayest be feared.
I wait for the Lord, my soul waits,
and in his word I hope;
   my soul waits for the Lord
   more than watchmen for the morning,
   more than watchmen for the morning.
O Israel, hope in the Lord!
For with the Lord there is steadfast love,
   and with him is plenteous redemption.
And he will redeem Israel from all his iniquities.

PSALM 130

Father of mercies,
   though I cannot fathom the murky depths
     that would give birth to such crimes
      I confess that I know all too well
       the darkness within my own soul
        and I too stand before you
         a debtor to your unsearchable mercy.
        Grant us grace to repent.
        Forgive us and heal us,
         Father of mercies.

Paul Thigpen

✦ For the Whole Church ✦

Almighty God, we beseech you to hasten to the aid of your Church. Let your mercy go before us, rather than your wrath, for if you take heed of all our iniquities, none of us will have strength to bear it. Pardon us sinners, then, lest you destroy the handiwork you have so lovingly created. Through Christ our Lord, *Amen.*

Lord, we beseech you, help your servants, whom you have redeemed with your precious Blood. Make them to be numbered with your saints in glory everlasting. Lord, save your people and bless your inheritance. Govern them and lift them up forever. Day by day we bless you and we praise your name forever, world without end. Vouchsafe, O Lord, this day to keep us without sin. Have mercy on us, O Lord, have mercy on us. Let your mercy, O Lord, be upon us, as we place our hope in you.

From the *Te Deum*

Savior and Lord, God of all flesh and Lord of all spirit, you who are blessed and the Source of blessing, sanctify our bishop, shield him from temptation, give him knowledge and wisdom, guide him in the ways of your truth.

We entreat you also for his fellow clergy. Sanctify them, give them knowledge and wisdom, inspire their teaching, make them true and blameless ministers of your holy gospel. To all clergymen in Holy Orders grant your peace and mercy; help them to advance in holiness.

We pray to you also for all religious. Guide their footsteps along sinless paths, enable them to shape the whole course of their lives in holiness and purity.

Bless the laity. Have mercy on all families, fathers, mothers, and children. Be with all those who are single. Give them your blessing, so that they may all advance in virtue and live as you would have them live.

Through Jesus Christ our Lord, *Amen.*

Lord God of Ages, you who reveal yourself in heaven to the pure in heart and on earth dwell in the Church, you who are served by holy angels and pure souls who from heaven form a living choir for the praise and glory of truth: Grant that this Church of yours may be a living Church, a Church unspotted and full of godly virtues, peopled with ministers worthy to sing your praise. We pray to you for all members of this Church. Have mercy upon them, forgive them all, and pardon all their sins. Give them grace not to sin again. Be a tower of strength to them, withstanding all temptation. Have pity on every man, woman, and child; reveal yourself in each one; and let knowledge of you be written in their hearts, through Jesus Christ your only-begotten Son. Through him be power and glory to you in the Holy Spirit, now and for evermore, *Amen.*

O God, you are a good Shepherd to have given us your only-begotten Son to be our true Shepherd. In obedience to you, he laid down his life for your little sheep and made of his blood a bath for us.... Your servants are asking you through this blood to show mercy to the world and to make Holy Church blossom again with the fragrant flowers of good, holy shepherds whose perfume will dispel the stench of the rotting evil flowers.

You have said, eternal Father, that because of your love for your creatures, and through the intercession and innocent sufferings of your servants, you would show mercy to the world by reforming Holy Church, thus giving us refreshment. Wait no longer, then, to turn toward us the eye of mercy. Since it is your will to answer us even before we call to you, answer now in your voice of mercy....

You created us out of nothing. Now that we exist, be merciful to us and remake the vessels you have created and crafted in your image and likeness. Reform them by grace in the mercy and blood of your Son. *Amen.*

St. Catherine of Siena, *Dialogue*

IV: Responses From Church Officials

"APPALLING SIN IN THE EYES OF GOD"

Address of Pope John Paul II to the Cardinals of the United States and Conference Officers

On Tuesday, April 23, 2002, at the end of the morning session of the emergency meeting of American cardinals in Rome, the Holy Father addressed the gathering.

Dear Brothers,

1. Let me assure you first of all that I greatly appreciate the effort you are making to keep the Holy See, and me personally, informed regarding the complex and difficult situation which has arisen in your country in recent months. I am confident that your discussions here will bear much fruit for the good of the Catholic people of the United States. You have come to the house of the Successor of Peter, whose task it is to confirm his brother bishops in faith and love, and to unite them around Christ in the service of God's people. The door of this house is always open to you. All the more so when your communities are in distress.

Like you, I too have been deeply grieved by the fact that priests and religious, whose vocation it is to help people live holy lives in the sight of God, have themselves caused such suffering scandal to the young. Because of the great harm done by some priests and religious, the Church herself is viewed with distrust, and many are offended at the way in which the Church's leaders are perceived to have acted in this matter. The abuse which has caused this crisis is by every standard wrong and rightly considered a crime by society; it is also an appalling sin in the eyes of God. To the victims and their families, wherever they may be, I express my profound sense of solidarity and concern.

2. It is true that a generalized lack of knowledge of the nature of the problem and also at times the advice of clinical experts led bishops to make decisions which subsequent events showed to be wrong. You are now working to establish more reliable criteria to ensure that such mistakes are not repeated. At the same time, even while recognizing how indispensable these criteria are, we cannot forget the power of Christian conversion, that radical decision to turn away from sin and back to God, which reaches to the depths of a person's soul and can work extraordinary change.

Neither should we forget the immense spiritual, human, and social good that the vast majority of priests and religious in the United States have done and are still doing. The Catholic Church in your country has always promoted human and Christian values with great vigor and generosity, in a way that has helped to consolidate all that is noble in the American people. A great work of art may be blemished, but its beauty remains; and this is a truth which any intellectually honest critic will recognize. To the Catholic communities in the United States, to their pastors and members, to the men and women religious, to teachers in Catholic universities and schools, to American missionaries in all parts of the world, go the wholehearted thanks of the entire Catholic Church and the personal thanks of the Bishop of Rome.

3. The abuse of the young is a grave symptom of a crisis affecting not only the Church but society as a whole. It is a deep-seated crisis of sexual morality, even of human relationships, and its prime victims are the family and the young. In addressing the problem of abuse with clarity and determination, the Church will help society to understand and deal with the crisis in its midst. It must be absolutely clear to the Catholic faithful, and to the wider community, that bishops and

superiors are concerned, above all else, with the spiritual good of souls. People need to know that there is no place in the priesthood and religious life for those who would harm the young. They must know that bishops and priests are totally committed to the fullness of Catholic truth on matters of sexual morality, a truth as essential to the renewal of the priesthood and the episcopate as it is to the renewal of marriage and family life.

4. We must be confident that this time of trial will bring a purification of the entire Catholic community, a purification that is urgently needed if the Church is to preach more effectively the Gospel of Jesus Christ in all its liberating force. Now you must ensure that where sin increased, grace will all the more abound [see Rom 5:20]. So much pain, so much sorrow must lead to a holier priesthood, a holier episcopate, and a holier Church.

God alone is the source of holiness, and it is to him above all that we must turn for forgiveness, for healing, and for the grace to meet this challenge with uncompromising courage and harmony of purpose. Like the Good Shepherd of last Sunday's Gospel, pastors must go among their priests and people as men who inspire deep trust and lead them to restful waters [see Ps 23:2]. I beg the Lord to give the bishops of the United States the strength to build their response to the present crisis upon the solid foundations of faith and upon genuine pastoral charity for the victims, as well as for the priests and the entire Catholic community in your country. And I ask Catholics to stay close to their priests and bishops, and to support them with their prayers at this difficult time.

The peace of the Risen Christ be with you!

"A CALL TO GREATER FIDELITY"

The Final Communiqué of the American Cardinals at Rome

On April 23-24, 2002, an extraordinary meeting was held in the Vatican between the cardinals of the United States and the leadership of the United States Conference of Catholic Bishops and the heads of several offices of the Holy See on the subject of the sexual abuse of minors. The meeting was called with three goals in mind:

- on the part of the American bishops, to inform the Holy See about the difficulties which they have faced in recent months;
- on the part of the Roman Dicasteries, to hear directly from the American cardinals and the chief officials of the United States Conference of Catholic Bishops a general evaluation of the situation;
- and together to develop ways to move forward in addressing these issues.

As is known, the Holy Father received the working group in his private library late in the morning of Tuesday, April 23, and gave a programmatic address. Today, at the end of the morning session, His Holiness invited the American cardinals and bishops to lunch, to continue their discussion of some of the themes raised at the meeting.

The participants first of all wish to express their unanimous gratitude to the Holy Father for his clear indications of direction and commitment for the future. In communion with the Pope they reaffirm certain basic principles:

1) The sexual abuse of minors is rightly considered a crime by society and is an appalling sin in the eyes of God, above all when it is perpetrated by priests and religious whose vocation is to help persons to lead holy lives before God and men.

2) There is a need to convey to the victims and their families a profound sense of solidarity and to provide appropriate assistance in recovering faith and receiving pastoral care.

3) Even if the cases of true pedophilia on the part of priests and religious are few, all the participants recognized the gravity of the problem. In the meeting, the quantitative terms of the problem were discussed, since the statistics are not very clear in this regard. Attention was drawn to the fact that almost all the cases involved adolescents and therefore were not cases of true pedophilia.

4) Together with the fact that a link between celibacy and pedophilia cannot be scientifically maintained, the meeting reaffirmed the value of priestly celibacy as a gift of God to the Church.

5) Given the doctrinal issues underlying the deplorable behavior in question, certain lines of response have been proposed:

  a) the pastors of the Church need clearly to promote the correct moral teaching of the Church and publicly to reprimand individuals who spread dissent and groups which advance ambiguous approaches to pastoral care;
  b) a new and serious Apostolic Visitation of seminaries and other institutes of formation must be made without delay, with particular

emphasis on the need for fidelity to the Church's teaching, especially in the area of morality, and the need for a deeper study of the criteria of suitability of candidates to the priesthood.

c) it would be fitting for the bishops of the United States Conference of Catholic Bishops to ask the faithful to join them in observing a national day of prayer and penance, in reparation for the offenses perpetrated and in prayer to God for the conversion of sinners and the reconciliation of victims.

6) All the participants have seen this time as a call to a greater fidelity to the mystery of the Church. Consequently they see the present time as a moment of grace. While recognizing that practical criteria of conduct are indispensable and urgently needed, we cannot underestimate, in the words of the Holy Father, "the power of Christian conversion, that radical decision to turn away from sin and back to God, which reaches the depths of a person's soul and can work extraordinary change." At the same time, as His Holiness also stated, "People need to know that there is no place in the priesthood and religious life for those who would harm the young. They must know that bishops and priests are totally committed to the fullness of Catholic truth on matters of sexual morality, a truth as essential to the renewal of the priesthood and the episcopate as it is to the renewal of marriage and family life."

Again in the Holy Father's words, "neither should we forget the immense spiritual, human and social good that the vast majority of priests and religious in the United States have done and are still doing. The Catholic Church in your country has always promoted human and Christian values with great vigor and generosity, in a way that has helped to consolidate all that is noble in the American people. A great work of art may be blemished, but its beauty remains; and this is a truth which any intellectually honest critic will recognize. To the Catholic communities in the United States, to their pastors and members, to the men and women religious, to teachers in Catholic universities and schools, to American missionaries in all parts of the world, go the wholehearted thanks of the entire Catholic Church and the personal thanks of the Bishop of Rome."

For this reason, the cardinals and bishops present at the meeting today sent a message to all the priests of the United States, their co-workers in the pastoral ministry.

As part of the preparation for the June meeting of the American bishops, the United States participants in the Rome meeting presented to the prefects of the Roman Congregations the following proposals:

(1) We propose to send the respective Congregations of the Holy See a set of national standards which the Holy See will properly review (*recognitio*), in which essential elements for policies dealing with the sexual abuse of minors in dioceses and religious institutes in the United States are set forth.

(2) We will propose that the United States Conference of Catholic Bishops recommend a special process for the dismissal from the clerical state of a priest who has become notorious and is guilty of the serial, predatory, sexual abuse of minors.

(3) While recognizing that the Code of Canon law already contains a judicial process for the dismissal of priests guilty of sexually abusing minors, we will also propose a special process for cases which are not notorious but where the diocesan bishop considers the priest a threat

for the protection of children and young people, in order to avoid grave scandal in the future and to safeguard the common good of the Church.

(4) We will propose an Apostolic Visitation of seminaries and religious houses of formation, giving special attention to their admission requirements and the need for them to teach Catholic moral doctrine in its integrity.

(5) We will propose that the bishops of the United States make every effort to implement the challenge of the Holy Father that the present crisis "must lead to a holier priesthood, a holier episcopate, and a holier Church" by calling for deeper holiness in the Church in the United States, including ourselves as bishops, the clergy, the religious, and the faithful.

(6) We propose that the bishops of the United States set aside a day for prayer and penance throughout the Church in the United States, in order to implore reconciliation and the renewal of ecclesial life.

From the Vatican, April 24, 2002

"THE HEAVY BURDEN OF SORROW AND SHAME"

Message of the Cardinals of the United States to the Priests of the United States

On April 24, 2002, at the end of the interdicasterial meeting of the American leadership with the Holy Father and the cardinals, heads of Congregations and Councils, the cardinals and leadership of the bishops' conference published the following message for priests.

We, the cardinals of the United States and the presidency of the National Conference of Catholic Bishops, gathered with our brother cardinals of the Roman Curia around the Successor of Peter, wish to speak a special word to you, our brother priests who give yourselves so generously from day to day in service of God's people. At our meeting, you have been very much in our minds and hearts, for we know the heavy burden of sorrow and shame that you are bearing because some have betrayed the grace of ordination by abusing those entrusted to their care. We regret that episcopal oversight has not been able to preserve the Church from this scandal. The entire Church, the Bride of Christ, is afflicted by this wound—the victims and their families first of all, but also you who have dedicated your lives to "the priestly service of the Gospel of God" [see Rom 15:16].

To all of you we express our deep gratitude for all that you do to build up the body of Christ in holiness and love. We pledge to support you in every possible way through these troubled times, and we ask that you stay close to us in the bond of the priesthood as we make every effort to bring the healing grace of Christ to the people whom we serve.

We are in complete harmony with the Holy Father when he said in his address yesterday: "Neither should we forget the immense spiritual, human, and social good that the vast majority of priests and religious in the United States have done and are still doing.... To the Catholic communities in the United States, to their pastors and members, to the men and women religious, to teachers in Catholic universities and schools, to American missionaries in all parts of the world, go the wholehearted thanks of the entire Catholic Church and the personal thanks of the Bishop of Rome."

As we look to the future, let us together beg the eternal High Priest for the grace to live this time of trial with courage and confidence in the Crucified Lord. This echoes the summons of our ordination: "Imitate the mystery you celebrate; model your life on the mystery of the Lord's cross" (*Rite of Ordination*); and it is a vital part of what we now offer the Church as she passes through this time of painful purification. From the house of the Successor of Peter, who has confirmed us in our faith, we wish in turn to confirm you in the humble and exalted service of the Catholic priesthood to which we have been called. Peace be with you!

A CATHOLIC RESPONSE TO SEXUAL ABUSE
Confession, Contrition, Resolve

Bishop Wilton D. Gregory

Bishop Wilton D. Gregory of Belleville, Illinois, is the president of the United States Conference of Catholic Bishops. This is the text of his Presidential Address presented at the annual meeting of the bishops in Dallas, Texas, June 13, 2002.

My brother bishops, my brothers and sisters in Christ:

The Catholic Church in the United States is in a very grave crisis, perhaps the gravest we have faced. This crisis is not about a lack of faith in God. In fact, those Catholics who live their faith actively day by day will tell you that their faith in God is not in jeopardy; it has indeed been tested by this crisis, but it is very much intact. The crisis, in truth, is about a profound loss of confidence by the faithful in our leadership as shepherds, because of our failures in addressing the crime of the sexual abuse of children and young people by priests and Church personnel. What we are facing is not a breakdown in belief, but a rupture in our relationship as bishops with the faithful. And this breakdown is understandable. We did not go far enough to ensure that every child and minor was safe from sexual abuse. Rightfully, the faithful are questioning why we failed to take the necessary steps.

The unity for which the Lord prayed fervently for his disciples and his Church on the night before he died—a unity that sadly has been broken too often in our history as a Church—is in serious danger of being fractured again, this time within our beloved Church in the United States.

These are times that cry out for a genuine reconciliation within the

221

Church in our country, not a reconciliation that merely binds a wound so that we can move forward together in some hobbled kind of fashion. What we need is a reconciliation that heals: one that brings us together to address this issue in a way that ensures that it will not happen again; one that begins with a love of the Truth that is Jesus Christ; one that embraces fully and honestly the authentic elements of the Sacrament of Penance as we celebrate it in the Catholic tradition. Only by truthful confession, heartfelt contrition, and firm purpose of amendment can we hope to receive the generous mercy of God and the forgiveness of our brothers and sisters.

Confession

The penance that is necessary here is not the obligation of the Church at large in the United States, but the responsibility of the bishops ourselves. Both "what we have done" and "what we have failed to do" contributed to the sexual abuse of children and young people by clergy and Church personnel. Moreover, our God-given duty as shepherds of the Lord's people holds us responsible and accountable to God and to the Church for the spiritual and moral health of all of God's children, especially those who are weak and most vulnerable. It is we who need to confess; and so we do.

We are the ones, whether through ignorance or lack of vigilance, or—God forbid—with knowledge, who allowed priest abusers to remain in ministry and reassigned them to communities where they continued to abuse. We are the ones who chose not to report the criminal actions of priests to the authorities, because the law did not require this. We are the ones who worried more about the possibility of scandal than in bringing about the kind of openness that helps prevent abuse. And we are the ones who, at times, responded to victims and their families as adversaries and not as suffering members of the Church.

Contrition

Our confession is matched by a heartfelt contrition.

To the victim-survivors, I want to say this. If we bishops have learned anything, it is how devastating are the effects of sexual abuse on the children and young people who suffer it. Even the passage of many years does not wipe away the memory of these terrible crimes. And so often, beyond the wounds inflicted on the memory, a person's whole personality also shows the results of these violations of innocence. Those of us who have not experienced sexual abuse in our childhood can never fully understand what it has done to you. But I promise you this: We bishops will make every effort to take on your perspective, to see the world and the Church through your eyes, and to look at our own actions over the last decade from your point of view.

More importantly, in my own name and in the name of all of the bishops, I express the most profound apology to each of you who have suffered sexual abuse by a priest or another official of the Church. I am deeply and will be forever sorry for the harm you have suffered. We ask your forgiveness.

To the parents and families of the victim-survivors, I want to say this. God has blessed the bond between a husband and wife in the Church as a sacrament, as a real sign of his abiding presence in your marriage. The fullest blessing that God can give you in your marriage is the gift of children. In the act of parenting, you become partners with God in the creation of new life, and your family becomes a "domestic church" where your children first hear the gospel of the Lord Jesus. You have a great responsibility.

But how can we bishops dare to look you parents in the eye and tell you that your children are your greatest treasure if we do not also treasure, love, and protect them? I promise you this: Following the example of the Lord Jesus, today we bishops recommit ourselves to placing the protection of your children first, and I am confident that the work we will do together over the next few days here in Dallas and every day thereafter will confirm that promise with solid action to provide for the safety of your children in the Church.

As a prelude to that work, in my own name and in the name of all of the bishops, I express a profound apology to each of you who have children or family members who have suffered sexual abuse by a priest or another representative of the Church. I am deeply and will be forever sorry for the harm that you have suffered as a parent or loved one of a victim-survivor. We ask your forgiveness.

I need to say a word to the deacons, the religious, and the laity. These past few months have been a time of enormous challenge and heartbreak for you. We bishops are deeply aware of the confusion and the disillusionment that you have experienced because of failures in our leadership. We know that these have been especially difficult times for those of you who serve the Church in religious institutes, in parishes and schools, and in the many social works of the Church throughout our country.

To each of you—and in the name of all the bishops—I offer a profound apology for the hurt and the embarrassment you have suffered. We ask your forgiveness.

I also want to express to the deacons, religious, and laity our deepest gratitude for the faithful way in which you have continued your generous service in and your love of the Church despite the pain you have felt. Your selfless service to the Church and to society is vital to the good of the human community and to the Church. In a special way, I want you to know how grateful we bishops are for the loving support you have continued to show to our good priests. They have told us often how much your care and concern means to them.

To our faithful priests, I want to say this on behalf of the bishops. The Holy Spirit in the Sacrament of Orders unites us to you as our first collaborators in ministry, and we love you as brothers. We are also proud of and grateful for the selfless way in which you serve the Lord and your brothers and sisters day after day. We bishops are profoundly sorry that mistakes we have made in dealing with priest-abusers have caused some to call into question your own good name and your reputation as priests. We are also sorry that failures in our leadership have led to a breakdown of trust between priests and bishops, brothers in ministry. We ask your forgiveness.

I ask our priests to continue to work closely with us; we need you. Let us, together, ask God to grant us the grace we need for a full renewal of the priesthood and the episcopate in this country to genuine holiness of life and Christ-like service. This is what the Lord asks of us. The Church deserves nothing less.

My brother bishops: There is a lot of anger among us in this room—righteous anger. Since 1985—as a Conference and individually as diocesan bishops—we have been working on the problem of sexual abuse to ensure, as much as is humanly possible, that the Church would be a safe environment for our children. In 1992, after seven years of study and work that included listening sessions with victim-survivors and other members of the Church, consultations with experts, and experimentation with policies on the diocesan level, we together adopted "Five Principles to Follow in Dealing with Accusations of Sexual Abuse." The vast majority of bishops embraced these principles, made them the standard for policies on sexual abuse in their dioceses and, therefore, contributed effectively to the protection of children in the Church. These policies, however, were not implemented effectively in every diocese across this country.

In a matter of a few months, this has become painfully clear. The very solid and good work that has been accomplished by the majority of bishops in their dioceses has been completely overshadowed by the imprudent decisions of a small number of bishops during the past ten years. It is as if the fabric of the good work that has been accomplished had never existed or had completely unraveled. The anger over this is very real and very understandable. I know. I feel it myself. But I cannot remain there. And neither can any of you. I offer two suggestions, two challenges, really.

First: In your own name and in mine, I have been asking for a lot of forgiveness this morning. From the victim-survivors. From the parents and families of the victim-survivors. From the deacons, the religious, and the laity. And from our priests. The reconciliation and healing that we need at this moment in the life of the Church in this country will never happen unless God's grace provides a flood of forgiveness. Let us be models of forgiveness to one another. I believe that the grace for us to forgive one another is there. Let us each in our hearts ask God for the measure we need. He will not disappoint.

Second: May I suggest that we use the energy that could so easily fuel our anger in a thoroughly constructive way to complete the work that we have come to Dallas to accomplish. We have much to do, and little time in which to do it. We need to put aside that which could distract us and set our sights solely on the task at hand: a full and recommitted effort towards the protection of our children and young people. Together we must ensure that every child in America is protected from sexual abuse by a priest or any representative of the Church.

Resolve

The resolve that we bishops bring to the work before us is nourished by a firm purpose of amendment. The failures of the past must not be repeated. Having faced and acknowledged our mistakes and expressed heartfelt sorrow for those failures, we bishops need to complete, once and for all, the work we began together almost twenty years ago to make our Church as safe an environment as is humanly possible for our children and young people.

In order that our work might be on the surest footing, having dealt as honestly with the past as we are able, I would like to speak a brief word to three groups of people.

To victim-survivors: If there is anyone who has been a victim of sexual abuse by a priest or representative of the Church in the United States and has not yet reported this fact, I ask you to report it to the bishop of your diocese and to the appropriate civil authorities. Though this may be a very difficult step for you, the Church does love you and wants to help you find justice and healing.

To priests: If there is any priest who is responsible for the crime of the sexual abuse of a child or young person and your bishop is not aware of this fact, I ask you to come forward to your bishop and report this fact so that justice and the Church will be served, and you will be able to live honestly with your own conscience.

To my brother bishops: If there is any bishop who has sexually abused a child or young person, I ask you to report this fact to the Nunciature so that justice and the Church will be served, and you will be able to live honestly with your own conscience.

During the past five months the sexual abuse of children and young people, especially by priests, has been a focus of the national and local media. In my own many encounters with the media, I have been treated usually, if not invariably, with consideration. I have a great respect for the power of the media to do good. If, as seems to be the case, the current attention of the media has helped victims of abuse to come forward, this has been a great service. I am particularly pleased that the media have also given greater attention recently to the issue of the sexual abuse of children and young people as a societal problem.

But I ask the media to allow me a moment of complete candor. During these last months, the image of Catholic hierarchy in this country has been distorted to an extent which I would not have thought possible six months ago. Sad and disturbing facts, often long in the past, have been readily presented in ways that create an erroneous image of the Church in 2002 as neglectful and uncaring in a matter about which we bishops have cared a great deal for many years now.

The advances we have made in trying to overcome the problem of the sexual abuse of children and young people have not been so quickly reported: more stringent screening of seminary candidates, seminary formation that makes healthy human development a major goal, and procedures to remove from ministry those who have proved a threat to children and young people.

I am not only proud to defend this body from the distortions; I do it as a matter of justice to set the record straight so that the work we bishops will be doing today and tomorrow will be seen in its proper perspective—as an important piece of work that we have been doing together for twenty years. There has indeed been some very thoughtful media coverage and editorial analysis alongside the hysterical and distorted coverage, analysis which has provided real insight into the issues. We bishops accept the challenge of this insightful coverage to do better in the fulfillment of our responsibilities. As we accept that challenge, I count on you, the media, to report fully and fairly on what we do these days and in the days and years to come.

When all is said and done, the Catholic Church in the United States remains the single largest private provider of services, care, formation, and education for children throughout this nation. And we do that service well, effectively, and from the hearts of very faithful people. You who serve in the media have challenged us bishops well by calling us to better action in the fulfillment of our responsibilities. I extend the same courtesy to you and challenge you to do the same in the fulfillment of your own responsibilities.

The task that we bishops have before us these days in Dallas is enormous and daunting. We are called to put into place policies that will insure the full protection of our children and young people and to bring an end to sexual abuse in the Church. This we will do. Sadly, however, no decisions or policies that we make or put in place can save our children from human depravity. Our actions will have to be matched by an uncommon and persistent vigilance.

As we set about this task, we bishops are very conscious of the fact that we were not able to come to this moment alone, nor will we be able to complete it alone. We realize, as perhaps never before, our corporate need for and this grace-filled opportunity of working more collaboratively with our devoted laity, religious, and clergy. We have very much relied on the voices that have chosen to be helpful from within and outside of the Church. On behalf of the bishops, I want to thank the so many people who have written or called us to offer insights about how we might deal with the issue of sexual abuse within the Church. We are deeply grateful for your assistance, and I can promise you that we will be looking for it to continue in the future as we explore new ways to insure the protection of our children and young people.

It is my fervent hope that the successful work we do in the Church to address sexual abuse will be of great assistance to our society at large. It is no secret among those who have responsibility for children that the issue of the sexual abuse of children and young people is one which plagues all sectors of our society. I look forward to exploring creative ways in which we might work more fully and effectively with other groups in our society towards strengthening the protection of children.

These have been months and years and decades of tremendous suffering and pain, especially for the victim-survivors and their families, but also for so many others in the Church. I renew my faith in the words of St. Paul, "where sin has increased, grace has far surpassed it," [Romans 5:20] and I invite each of you to do the same. In Jesus Christ there is no cross without resurrection; no death without life; no purgation without cleansing and grace. Let us embrace the grace that God gives us so abundantly, so that the work we do in these days together may be to his glory and contribute to full reconciliation and healing in the Church.

God bless each of you!